Treasures of Darkness

"I will give thee the treasures of darkness, and hidden riches of secret places"
(Isaiah 45:3).

The light pierces the darkness as the glory of the resurrection of the indwelling Christ is revealed in us. Our precious humanity is then anointed with the righteousness which is of God, by faith."

Published by
Christ, Our Life Ministries, Inc.

Copyright © 1997
Sylvia D. Pearce

All rights reserved. No part of this book may be reproduced in any form, except for the inclusion of brief quotations in a review, without permission in writing from the author or publisher.

Published by: Christ, Our Life Ministries, Inc.
P.O. Box 43268
Louisville, Kentucky 40253-0268

Eighth Edition
Eighth Printing • 1000 • December 2006

ISBN: 978-0-9714381-0-1

Additional copies are available. See the back of this book for information

Printed in the USA by

3212 East Highway 30 • Kearney, NE 68847 • 1-800-650-7888

Dedication

This book is dedicated with deepest love and gratitude to my close friend, Alan Parker, an attorney in Knoxville, Tennessee. It was his groundbreaking talk on the mystery of darkness being transmuted into light by the Seven-Fold-Spirits of God that revolutionized my understanding. This revelation opened the door to a fuller meaning of the operation of the Cross by which God Himself died to His own self-seeking desire to be, and birthed into being His only begotten Son thereby becoming the "The Lamb slain before the foundation of the world." Alan also opened my understanding to the necessity of opposites, and how evil fits back into God. It was at a conference in Louisville, Kentucky in September of 1980 that Alan expounded on these mysteries, which were unlocked to him in the writings of the famous 16th century German mystic, Jacob Boehme. Alan capsulates these truths in a booklet still in print entitled "The Cross in The Heart of God."[1]

---

1. "The Cross in the Heart of God" by Alan Parker is available from the, "Christ, Our Life Ministries."

Contents

Foreword by: Norman P. Grubb

Chapters	Page
1. What is Man?	13.
2. My Friend Finds The Answer	18.
3. Eternal Life Is A Person	25.
4. Two Deliverances Available In The Cross	29.
5. Jesus Christ, The Human	33.
6. The Body Death ("Dead to the Sin")	37.
7. Romans Seven ("Dead to the Law")	42.
8. Not I, But Sin	46.
9. The Birth Of A New Consciousness	53.
10. A Severe Mercy	64.
11. Origin Of The Lie	74.
12. The Temptations Of Jesus	77.
13. Daily Weakness	81.
14. Temptation	84.
15. Simple Towards Evil	89.
16. Seeing Through Evil to God Only	93.
17. Calling Into Being That Which Does Not Exist	99.
18. Meaning Of Suffering	111.
19. Suffering Is Love In Disguise	117.
20. The Fellowship Of His Suffering	122.
21. My Uncle Bill	127.
22. Intercession	133.
23. God's Love Can Move Mountains	141.
24. Kings And Priests	149.
25. Prisoners Of Hope	155.
26. Precious Seeds	161.
27. Diane's Joy Bottle	165.
28. Susan, My Chariot Of Fire	169.
29. Postscript	173.

Acknowledgments

I wish to extend a heartfelt thanks to a number of friends for editing and scrutinizing this book while in manuscript form. Brian Coatney expertly edited it. Margo Sanders, Jenny Fienning, and Judy Dunn lovingly gilded the edges with their finishing golden touch while Linda Bunting and Harriet Wearren scrutinized it. I couldn't have done it without you. Thank you very much.

As a young Christian I sat under a godly woman and Bible teacher, Pauline Catlett. It was through her teaching that the Spirit revealed to me the blood of Christ, the grace of God, and what it means to take up our cross. She lived with a cross in her own life which certainly got the message through to me. I feel privileged to have known this precious saint whom I know is catching my love from Glory.

It was at Van and Pauline Catlett's house, soon after my conversion, that I fell heir to the most revolutionary teacher in our generation, Norman Grubb. I consider him the modern day Martin Luther and Paul of Tarsus wrapped into one. Norman pioneered and made palatable the Spirit's revelation of the second, and complete work of the cross, which is, "Christ in you, the hope of glory." In doing this he also unraveled the misconceptions concerning the human self found in Romans Seven so that like Paul, in Colossians 1:28, "we might present every man perfect in Christ."[1]

I was privileged to know Norman as a mentor, friend, and traveling companion for over 25 years. I want to thank him for the price he paid in order to minister to the world these tremendous revelations. Norman always said that he would be cheering us on from above and I know that he is. As I write this I am overwhelmed with thanksgiving at the Father purposing me to have known such great people.

I would like to acknowledge our dearest and closest friends, John and Linda Bunting and Wade and Harriet

Wearren, who traveled with Scott and me on this same quest of discovering our oneness with Christ. We have loved each other, taught each other, and share the same passion in sharing what has been revealed to us. We three couples are like the Ecclesiastical cord: "a threefold cord is not easily broken."

Finally, I would like to acknowledge my precious husband, Scott. Without his encouragement, love, and computer help I would have never written this book. He insisted on buying a computer long before I thought there was a need. I was reluctant and technologically ignorant. He patiently taught me how to use it, and now it has become my right arm. I thank him for the hours I have spent in my computer room while he has carried much of the family's load. He said to me one time after my frustration from numerous phone calls, "This house and it's work will always be here; helping God's people is what we are about and what is really important." We are truly a team with one mind and purpose.

The Lord has surely blessed me with His very best.

---

1. Most of Norman Grubb's books are still available from: "Christ, Our Life Ministries, P.O. Box 43268, Louisville, Kentucky, 40253-0268.

Foreword

These tremendous Biblical truths, which are laid out here are not known by the vast majority of born again believers, not to speak of those still without Christ. This teaching will become part of your inner being by the Word of God, and by the witness of the Spirit, if you are among the hungry who **must** find a total answer. You will be among those who, as Apollas, were taken aside by Aquila and Priscilla and "taught the way of God more perfectly." That same "perfect way" will be yours as the Spirit's light is fully lit in you where there are at present shadowy areas. It is the "Fullness of understanding." Paul wrote of it to the Ephesians, "the eyes of your understanding be enlightened; that you may know what the riches of the glory of his inheritance in the saints"(1:18). The Scriptures plainly give an answer to these questions deep in all of us: What is Man?; Who am I?; and How do I function as I am meant to? Where am I among those who bear much fruit and the fruit that remains, which Jesus said is the normal product of a branch in its vine (John 15:16)?

It must be understood that the full value of this teaching is for those to whom John 3:16 has become a reality. They as Jesus said, have been "born-again," and can "see the kingdom of God." Now, knowing they are a "new creation" in Christ and the Spirit bearing His fruit, they are concerned about those areas of failure and even sins in their lives. These teachings, therefore, are for those who "leaving the first principles of the doctrine of Christ" (Heb. 6:1) "seek to go on to perfection." Their sins have been blotted out by faith in the shed blood of Christ and they are justified by His resurrection. But now, what troubles them is the many discordant reactions of their self life and daily living.

So read it, chew it over, and look up the Scripture references. And as that fullness of liberating light is lit in you by the Word and Spirit, you will find yourselves among those who cannot hold their peace, like the prophets of old. You will have to be among us who are "driven" by the Spirit to share our "treasure" with all who are in our reach, and even beyond, because what we have belongs to every redeemed member of the body of Christ, and indeed to all those not yet in the body as they respond to the light.

Here is this piece of "heavenly treasure," which Sylvia herself sought, learned and received with fullness of light, combined with her special gift of being able to teach so clearly what is first her own "pearl of great price."[1]

Norman P. Grubb
(Missionary, Author and Founder-
General Secretary of the Worldwide
Evangelization Crusade)

---

1. Foreword written by Norman Grubb for, "What is Man?"(the forerunner to this book).

Preface

"But as for you, you thought evil against me; but God <u>meant</u> it for good, to bring to pass, as it is this day, to save much people alive."
(Genesis 50:20)

In this world, two prevailing unresolved problems confront mankind: man hates himself and man hates suffering. Ironically, God loves both man and man's suffering. Most of us spend our lives either trying to improve our imperfect selves, or trying to protect ourselves from what we think will cause us pain and suffering. Until we can see as God sees, know as God knows, and reconcile both ourselves as well as our sufferings back into God, we vainly grope in darkness without the light that can truly set us free.

We know God loves man. But why doesn't man love himself? And what do we believe about our sufferings? How can anyone say that God is pleased with suffering when most of us hate it so much? How do we reconcile the agony that is in this world with an all-loving God "who means **all** things after the council of his own will" (Eph. 1:11)?

These questions have been on the hearts of many a philosopher and seeker of the truth from the beginning of time. It is understandable that these questions are unanswered in the non-Christian world, but surprisingly they are generally unanswered in the Christian world as well.

In the "Treasures of Darkness," I want to share what God has revealed to my simple, but hungry heart. I have agonized for years to find answers to these questions for myself. My hope is that the truths revealed in this book will answer some of the same questions for you.

What really breaks my heart, and what precipitated this book is seeing Christians overwhelmed and defeated by evil circumstances in their lives. Most of the time, we Christians are either beating ourselves up for lack of faith, or for our lack of control over our "sinful" selves. We spiral downward with endless forms of self-examination, focusing all our attention on our failing, miserable selves. This self-analysis leaves us defeated, hopeless, and powerless.

My prayer is that Christians will learn the secret of how we can put our sufferings, as well as our failing disillusioned selves, back into God by faith. Only then can He transform our pain into glory and our "failing selves" into glorious liberated sons of God.

Mankind knows separation, wrath, and judgment, and rightly so, for these are the consequences of our disobedient and fallen state. But if we are to ever get our lives into focus and live as liberated Christian people, we will have to see all things as a part of God, and His loving purposed plan for our lives. If not, we are forever caught in the trap of double mindedness and are "unstable in all our ways."

When we know the secret of seeing that **all** things come from the hand of our loving heavenly Father, life becomes a thrilling adventure of looking into God's mysterious ways in which He is always meaning evil for our good (Genesis 50:20). If we will dare claim our rightful inheritance purchased by the precious blood and **body** of Jesus Christ, our double-minded consciousness will be transformed into the single eye of faith.

I have been compelled by an unceasing burden to share these wonderful liberating secrets that have freed me. As you read this book, don't try to understand it intellectually. If you do, you will miss the heart of what I am saying. Read it with your heart, for it was written from mine. Let the Holy Spirit speak to you with his still small voice, for **He alone can reveal these truths to you.**

1.
What is Man?

"What is man, that Thou dost take thought of him? And the son of man, that Thou dost care for him? Yet Thou hast made him a little lower than God (Elohim); thou dost crown him with glory and majesty! Thou dost make him to rule over the works of Thy hands;"
(Psalms 8:3-5).

Man, as well as the Son of man, is a simple container, just like a coffee cup. Our humanity is the cup, and Christ is the coffee, and these two are one cup <u>of</u> coffee. Look at how the New Testament describes our humanity: We are called **temples**, not the deity (I Corinthians 6:19-20); **vessels,** not the contents, (Romans 9:22-23); **branches**, not the vine (John 15:1); (Romans 6:21-22); **bodies**, not the head (Ephesian 1:22-23 & Colossians 1:18); **slaves**, not the master (Romans 6:17-18); and **wives,** not the husband (Romans 7:2-4). Let us look at what the function of these illustrations are: Temples are His **dwelling place**; Vessels **offer the liquid** they contain; Branches **reproduce the life** and fruit of the vine; Bodies are **operated by the head**; Slaves **do the work** of their owner; Wives **receive** the seed of their husbands.

The problem comes when we confuse the function of the two. We think we, "the temple," should act like the deity: we should produce "fruit" apart from the "Vine." We then resemble Ichobod Crane's headless horseman, a "body" acting apart from the "head." We believe we have independent freedom from God to "do our own thing," and then we think we should produce children apart from the seed of our Husband. These are the lies that permeate us and pose as the truth. The truth is that the human has no ability in himself to perform righteousness, yet we Christians spend years trying to be good and please God by our self-effort. No wonder we are so powerless! (2 Cor 12:9)

If only we could catch a glimpse of the truth of "What is man?" we would then see the real truth of our precious humanity and the veil covering our eyes would be removed. We are God's glorious creation, created in His very own image. The Pharisees took up stones when Jesus testified of man's glory. But Jesus unequivocally declared that even their own law witnesses of the fact that man is really a god: "**Ye are gods!**" (Psalms 82).

What does this verse mean? We Christians are so afraid of our humanity, we think, and are taught, that it is either evil in itself, in that we have sinful flesh, or that it is good (or God) by itself, which would be what New Age teaches. Because we have been so inundated with lies, we throw the baby (this verse) out with the bath water. Don't we understand that Satan can only pervert the truth; he cannot create anything new, for he is not the creator. "Ye are gods," is **God's** truth. Yet Satan perverts this truth by duping us humans into believing that we, of ourselves, are, or should be, the content in the cup. Therefore we **(the cup)** should try to be good, or, if we sin, **we** (the cup) should have the power to keep ourselves from sin. We are either proud and self-righteous for doing good, or condemming and blaming ourselves for falling short. These are both lies. The human is neither evil nor good in himself, for like the temple and the vessel, the human is **a neutral being** and has no independent nature of its own.

We were evil in our unsaved days only because we were indwelt by Satan who caused us to express **his** evil nature (Ephesians 2:2-3; and John 8:44). The Cross of Christ has set us free from that evil nature by replacing it with Christ's own nature of holiness. That is why Paul declares in Colossians 1:28, "We preach, warning every man and teaching every man in all wisdom; that we may present **every man perfect** in Christ Jesus." It isn't good enough to know that we have a perfect Christ in us and not know that **man** was made perfect as well.

Don't be afraid of the truth, for the truth will set you free. When Jesus said, "Ye are gods," He did not mean that we are the Divine Creator himself or content of the cup. What he does mean is that we are created little gods, as a derivative of God our Father, as Paul declares in Act 17:29, "the offspring of God," or simply His means of expressing His diety nature.

God so greatly loves his human creation that it cannot be measured, for He declared it "very good." He did not create any two things alike, for God loves variety, that is evident in nature. He loves our bodily forms, all so different in shape and color and size. He loves our various kinds of personalities: some sweet, others hard; some passive, some with tempers; some shy, some bold; and all others in between. For God cannot express His personhood through nature. A tree cannot express His other-love nature: only God's top creation and crowning glory, man, can unite with His divine Spirit and express His other-love nature.

Satan has stolen God's creation away to make unto himself a kingdom of servants, expressing his perverted nature of self-for-self. The rebellious satanic **"I will"** that first perverted Lucifer, infected mankind in the Garden and is the same **"I will"** that Paul struggled with, by trying not to covet in Romans Seven. And it is the same, **"not my will,** but Thine," that Jesus relinquished in the garden. This satanic **"I will"** is thankfully the same **"I"** that was crucified with Christ (Galatians 2:20) on the Cross two thousand years ago defeating the satanic rule in mankind.

Through the Cross, Jesus our High Priest, has gained our freedom by paying the ultimate price of His own life. "If the son therefore shall make you free, you shall be free indeed (John 8:36)." He not only represented us as sin, dying to it and replacing it with His righteousness (II Corinthians 5:17), but he gained freedom for our humanity as well. Romans 6:6 says, "Knowing this, that our old man is crucified with him, in order that **the body of sin** might be destroyed, that henceforth we should not serve sin."

There are two deliverances proclaimed in this verse. The first is an exchange of Spirits, the old sinful nature out and Christ, the new nature, in. Then secondly (and, by the way, the point of the verse) "that the body of sin might be destroyed." What is the "body of sin?" It is our misused humanity expressing all forms of sin. This misuse was done away with at the Cross of Christ, delivering us from every form of bodily addiction. If a person is a Christian, he is already delivered from alcoholism, co-dependency, sex addiction, and every form of perversion, whether he knows it or not. As Christians we really are free and have a great liberating inheritance in Christ. Yet we live as bound up prisoners waiting for the second coming, thinking that only then can we be free.

It is not good enough that God knows we are already positionally delivered, we must know it too. God may be satisfied by the blood of Christ, but **we** are not satisfied until **we know** our total deliverance. Otherwise, we live life like someone having millions of dollars in the bank but living only on pennies. Our problem is tied up in the misunderstanding of our precious humanity. We, the cup, think we should be more victorious, instead of seeing our only function is that of a helpless container of Someone else who has already won the battle. That Someone else **is** the power of the universe and the great "I Am."

The Man of God—

When God wants to fill a man, and skill a man, and drill a man, when God wants to mold a man to play the noblest part, when He yearns with all his heart to create so great and bold a man that all the world will be amazed,
    Watch his methods, watch his ways!
How he ruthlessly perfects whom he royally elects, how he hammers him and hurts him, with mighty blows converts him into trial shapes of clay which only God understands, till his tortured heart is crying and he lifts beseeching hands. How He bends but never breaks when his good he undertakes, then how He uses whom He chooses, and with every purpose fuses him, by every act induces him to try his splendor out; God knows what He's about."

Author Unknown

2.
My Friend Finds the Answer

"But without faith it is impossible to please Him: for he that cometh to God <u>must believe</u> that He is, and that He is a rewarder of them that diligently seek Him"
(Hebrews 11:6).

    I have a precious friend whom I met 15 years ago at a meeting we were both attending. Immediately our hearts were drawn to each other. Over the years, our families have been knit together in love, as we have visited and had fellowship with each other many times since then. He is a perfectionist, and like Paul, **had** to solve his self problem, or die. I want to share with you his amazing story.
    My friend had an insatiable quest for perfection which began twenty years ago in Campus Crusade. He decided that if he could memorize three verses a day then he could memorize the entire New Testament in seven years. Accomplishing this feat, would in his mind, mean that he would be perfect. After memorizing one third of the New Testament, it overwhelmed him and he gave up.
    Then the drive to perfect himself resurfaced in other forms. He went to Christian seminars over and over again trying to change himself. The patterns that they presented for Christian living killed him. He tried very hard to work the principles and make restitution for his past sins. A lot of what he learned was very good, but as he says, "most of it was

somewhat morbid." His quest to be God's perfect man drove him to the seminary, where he diligently studied Greek and Hebrew. However, because he couldn't live up to his own ideals, he left after a year and a half, angry and depressed. He, like every earnest Christian, had great passion and drive for righteousness, and rightly so, for I believe that it is the common heart cry of everyone who loves the Lord.

The teachings he had learned were not wrong in themselves, but as long as a person has Christ and a **"me"** to perfect, then he has a false self that is bound to make law from outer teaching. All outer teaching has the possibility of becoming law to us; doesn't the Bible itself appear law to some, and grace to others? Until we know what it means to be "dead to the law" (Romans 7:1-4) we are always bound by some outer teaching.

Finally he heard the liberating truth of who he is in Christ, and began to make a real turn away from perfectionism. He began to learn the walk of faith and experience release. Yet the final truth of his humanity was still unknown to him. He knew that Christ lived in him, but what about this human form? What was his responsibility as a human? The answer became clear when he understood the **function** of the container, the human.

My friend reminded me of Paul in Romans 7--his desire was right, but how to perform, he could only say, "I find not." After a few years, my friend began to refocus on Satan and sin. "What if I'm in sin, maybe it's unbelief?" He became centered in on himself which led to depression as he tried to deal with his feelings of dissatisfaction and anger. His quest led him to a Christian group which propagated the 12 step program of AA, Co-Dependency, Adult Children of Alcoholics, and other related programs as part of their answer for recovery and progress. Around and around he went into the whirlwind of self-analyzing--"Maybe if my father had not left us children, then I wouldn't be like I am...What were the dysfunctions in my family?...My temper is out of control, maybe if I believe hard enough I can be released...I have strong sexual pulls, maybe I'm a sex addict, could that be my hidden sin? How can I purge myself of sin?"

He got worse instead of better because he recreated a false world that had already been crucified in Christ. The more he saw how dysfunctional his family had been, the more he hated and loathed his past and himself. This way of restoration was not healing at all, because it re-created a false reality. The truth is that Christ has redeemed our past and designed it to work together for our good, not our destruction. The 12 step programs are somewhat spiritual in nature, but my friend made them just another formula. He got worse and worse trying to make the 12 steps work, as he analyzed and re-analyzed himself. Finally, in despair and anguish, he contemplated suicide.

There is a time appointed by the Father for each of us to be introspective and self-searching, for it is in the identity level that we have been so deceived. And it is right there in our self that we discover our true identity. That time is a radical and valuable time for the Spirit to teach us who we are not, which conditions us to see who we really are. The very nature of this darkness usually isolates us from friends and family. Only in darkness and aloneness can God unite our divided consciousness from a separated striving self, to a released freedom, that only a right self can experience. I learned years ago not to touch this sacred and holy time, for it is a severe mercy. The great mystics called it, **"The alone with the Alone."** This is a far cry from what is offered to us today through psychology.

It is amazing to me how much psychology has inundated the Christian Church as a means of perfection. I heard a man of God recently say, "Psychology is a diversion from the leap of faith." His call was for Christians to return to the simple faith of our Fathers: Abraham, Isaac, Jacob, David, Peter and Paul. Psychology leaves people majoring on their problems, instead of leaping into the solution. Christ risen as us is our only hope, yet we Christians are putting our hope in false fleshly answers. There is only one hope, and that is Christ in us (Col. 1:27).

The highest form of human mentality is rational understanding, and psychology elevates understanding as a solution to inner healing. If we can understand ourselves, then we can discover ways to master ourselves. This is still flesh trying to master itself through self-effort. God crumbles our false hopes by saying, "Flesh and blood cannot inherit the Kingdom of God" (I Corinthians 15:50). For it is: "Not by (our) might, nor by (our) power, but by my **Spirit** saith the Lord" (Zech. 4:6).

A friend of mine from England, Barbara Rodgerson, once wrote this in a letter to me: "The more I seemed to dig and explore on a psychological level, the more elusive the 'root' to my problem became. I was like an onion with endless peels and no end in sight. Just tear another layer and more strong odors appeared, and that smell, more often than not, reeked of shame. I had to finally give it all up in place of the finished work of the Cross, where I found my final resting place."

While psychology may help us get within hearing distance of the truth, it cannot satisfy our empty hearts. Faith requires us to leave understanding behind and leap into Christ as the redeemer of our past, and the perfection of our present-tense life. Sharon, a Christian friend of mine who is a social worker, said to me the other day, "A leap of faith requires a death to our understanding, while psychology explains our lives away." If faith alone was good enough for Jesus, Paul, John and Martin Luther, then it is good enough for me.

Although the 12 step program has truth in it, it cannot be our **deliverer**. For some people are making psychology their new religion and substitute deliverer. Let us not make more of the **process** than we do of the **person** of Christ. How can we analyze God's creation? We are too complex to compartmentalize. "What is man, that Thou are mindful of him? Or the Son of Man, that Thou visitest Him? Thou madest Him a little lower than the God; Thou crownedst Him with glory and honor, and didst set Him over the works of Thy hands" (Hebrews 2:6-8). We are made in His image, yet like the snowflake, none of us are alike. Only the Creator really knows His creation. Can't we trust the God who created us to put the fragmented pieces of our psyche back together? "Unless the Lord build the house, they labor in vain that build it" (Psalms 127:1).

Isn't it interesting that the Bible tells us that, "The body of sins has been done away with" (Romans 6:6) and, "they that are Christ's have crucified the flesh with its affections and lusts" (Galatians 5:24). Yet we try to work out of us what the Cross accomplished for us two thousand year ago. No wonder Paul calls the Galatians foolish and bewitched for trying to perfect themselves through self-effort.

What we need is a fresh approach to how this truth can become a living reality in us today. Only when we dare to "possess our possessions," by taking a quantum leap of faith, believing that we are right just as we are, can we say with David, "My heart is fixed, O God, my heart is fixed: I will sing and give praise" (Psalms 57:7).

Yet all of us try as my friend did, and in a since we **must try**, because the death of trying conditions us to see the final liberation of our precious humanity. Can we dare accept ourselves as having a right humanity and catch the glory of being **God's asset** instead of His liability? My friend has, but it took a great death to **his** way of perfection, his rational understanding, and his clever reasoning powers. Aren't we glad that God is more clever than we!

Finally, after trying to purge himself from supposed sin through psychology and self-analyzing, my friend ended up in a psychiatric ward on the verge of a nervous breakdown. Soon after this, I contacted him by phone. His first words to me after five years of no contact were, "I cannot be contrite enough before the Lord." His voice was so low that I thought he would collapse just talking to me. I simply asked him several questions. "Do you really think that you are in sin? Maybe the reason you cannot be contrite enough, is, because you haven't really sinned. What does your heart tell you?" "My heart?" he said, "I'm not sure--I've been in my head so much that I don't know." Then I asked him one last question that really started him thinking: "Haven't you searched yourself for sin enough; haven't you searched every fiber of your body?"

Soon after that he came for a visit, and the Spirit was not long in illuminating him to the truth: "It pleased God, who separated him from his mother's womb, and called him by his grace, to reveal his Son in him" (Galatians 1:15&26). My friend's past was perfectly designed by God and ordained as the perfect negative background to bring out the real truth and reveal the very Son of God in my friend's precious humanity.

All the while he had really been a kept person. God's faithfulness had kept him from sin, but not from temptation. I wonder how many of us are confessing sin because we are feeling so condemned, when all the time it is **temptation** we are experiencing. These grave clothes are the false guilt we take because we think we have a failing self that needs improvement. My friend finally learned the difference between sin and temptation. He was falsely assuming that negative responses could not be in the life of God, and therefore were sin. Didn't Jesus say, "My soul is exceedingly sorrowful unto death," yet we know that He never sinned. The good news that came to my friend after years of self-abasement was that negatives such as weakness and darkness are right, and not wrong as he previously supposed. He could finally accept himself as a **right self** with right weaknesses.

When he would feel depressed, I would say to him, "Well then, be depressed." Then when he would accept and not fight or try to figure himself out, he experienced a great release. When we embrace our negatives, it takes the bite out of Satan's temptations. What we fight, fights us. But when we praise the Lord and accept ourselves as right and relax, the inner word from the Lord comes naturally and easily in us.

My friend has truly walked through the valley of the shadow of death, but now he doesn't fear evil anymore. God has anointed him with the good news that he is a right self and is, by faith already perfect in Christ. "For by one offering he hath **perfected forever** them that are sanctified" (Hebrews 10:14). A great release came to him, which brought rest to his soul and powerfully quickened his spirit. His life is a tremendous testimony to the resurrection power of the Spirit which is ours by **faith alone**.

3.
Eternal Life is a Person

"He that hath the Son hath (Eternal) Life;"
(I John 5:12)

I call the book of John the **"I am"** book. Jesus never said that He would give us a little piece of himself called "the way, the truth, and the life." He didn't say he would give us a little bit of bread and it would be life to us. He didn't say that he would give us resurrection, or life, or living water, and these would help is have more of God. No, what he did strongly and emphatically declare was this: "**I am** the Word, **I am** the Light of the world, **I am** the Living Water, **I am** the Bread of Life, **I am** the Resurrection and the Life, **I am** the Way, **I am** the Truth, and **I am** Eternal Life." God's name always has been "**I AM,**" not, "I have it to give." We do not have a distant God, dishing out to us humans, little bits of himself to live on. No, He has given us the fullness of Himself.

The mystery of the gospel is, "**Christ** in you, our only hope of glory" (Colossians 1:27). **He** is the deity in the temple, **He** is the contents of the vessel, **He** is the vine of the branch, **He** is the husband of the wife, and **He** is the head of the body. He firmly announced to all His creation, "My glory will I not give to another"(Isaiah 42:8). Therefore, salvation is a Person, Love is a Person, the Truth is a Person, Peace is a Person, Righteousness is a Person, and Eternal Life is not just a place we go after death, but it is a Person! His plan from the beginning was to create a family of sons who would freely contain and express **His** deity nature throughout eternity.

It takes a great blow to our egos to really know that we are only the clay pots and not the glory of the contents. Christ is the content, it is **He** that fills the temple. Yet we have been falsely taught that **we** are the one who should fulfill the law and try to fill our temples with good works. **The essence of all idolatry is trying to be what only God is.** This too is the essence of legalism. Trying to be good leaves our hearts empty and still crying out for more. For it is **Christ** who can fulfill the law in us, and it is He that wants the glory. We are **His** dwelling place, not our own dwelling place.

Could this be why Christians are so miserable? We, of all people, who know that our sins are forgiven and our future destination is heaven, should live in the joy of the Lord most of the time. But do we? I dare say that if we are honest, most of us experience the very opposite. I believe that most of us live condemned and frustrated lives, trying to cope with what we have and wonder why faith doesn't work. That is why so many Christians are crying out to Jesus, "Come quickly Lord Jesus," as they wait to be relieved from their misery by the second coming of Christ.

Our salvation and entrance into the kingdom of God is wonderful, but it's not good enough to just know that our sins are forgiven. What about now? What about the present tense? Why do we love the Jesus who saves us, but hate the human person that He saved? Did He do only half the work? Maybe we are getting closer to our answer by looking at just that. We think that **we** are responsible for finishing or perfecting the other half of what doesn't seem complete, namely us. What a job!

We are taught to pray more, read our Bibles more, come to Church more, tithe more, and strive to become more like Jesus. Then there is the problem of the world: we should keep ourselves from worldly thoughts and not overindulge in worldly pleasures such as eating, drinking, smoking, and carousing. Then there are our personal shortcomings: tempers, jealousies, pride, and secret sins. The list goes on forever. But most of all we must look good to the world and keep our reputations and God's reputation respectable because we must be good witnesses. I say it again, "What a job!"

Why doesn't Christianity work? I'm not happy and I'm not satisfied--God is satisfied because He sees his son in me, but **I'm not satisfied**. I look most of the time like Paul in Romans Seven--"the good that I would I do not: but the evil which I would not that I do. For the will is present with me; but how to perform that which is good I find not."

Since the problem is exposed in Romans seven, then the whole solution, which is the missing link in Christianity, is hidden there as well. The real problem and hidden sin of the Christian is self-effort. **"I ought to. I should do better by self-effort."** It is very subtle, though, for it seems right and good, yet in truth it is the very heart of our problem. The law continually stirs up self-effort because we believe we can and should do it. We are not believing in God, but in **ourselves**. Colossians 1:27 says, "To whom God would make known what is the riches of the glory of this mystery among the Gentiles; which is **Christ in you**, the hope of glory." The mystery of the Gospel is "Christ in you," yet we believe more in our own performance than Christ in us. That is why the third person of the Trinity (the Holy Spirit) is the least known to most Christians. We are provided with the life of Christ by the Holy Spirit, yet we strive in our own efforts **to be** that life.

Paul strongly warned the Galatians against legalism in their church. They began their Christian walk by faith alone, but soon after, added all kinds of laws to live by. Therefore, Paul cried out, "O foolish Galatians, who has **bewitched** you that you should **not obey** the truth. This only would I learn of you; Did you receive the Spirit by the works of the law, or the hearing of faith? Are you so foolish? Having begun in the Spirit, are you now made perfect by the flesh"(Galatians 3:1-3)? Paul's strong warning "Who has **bewitched you,**" implies that the devil is at work. It is devilish to try to become what only God himself is.

Let us understand though, that the law isn't wrong in itself, for it is God's perfect picture of His holy nature. Our problem is not God's picture of himself, the problem is how to be like that picture. We can never be like God by self-effort, yet God wants us to come to the end of believing that **"WE"** can do it. The only way that we can come to the end is for us to go right on trying. But don't try half way. Try with all your heart. Try until you're bloody from trying.

Most Christians settle somewhere in-between; a little bit of Jesus, a little bit of me, a little bit of the law, a little bit of righteousness, a little bit of the devil, a little bit of sin, "Ho hum! God doesn't expect me to be perfect anyway." On the contrary, Jesus demands perfection, "Be ye therefore perfect, even as your Father which is in heaven is perfect" (Matt. 5:48). Jesus says it has to be all or nothing. It is better to try until we can't try anymore, than to settle somewhere in the middle ground.

That is why Jesus said to the Laodiceian church in the book of Revelation, that because they were lukewarm and neither cold nor hot, He would spew them out of his mouth (Rev. 3:15-16). God wants self-effort to become exceedingly sinful. God wants you to be real desperate, so desperate that you can't try anymore. Then you are more than happy for righteousness not to depend on you. It is a desperate, but thankful heart, that knows that righteousness and eternal Life are both a person, and that person is Christ, who lives in us.

4.
Two Deliverances Available at the Cross

"For if, when we were enemies, we were reconciled to God by the death of His Son much more, being reconciled, we shall be saved by His life" (Romans 5:10).

There is a section in the book of John that really catches my attention. It is where Jesus says, "I am the bread of life: he that comes to me shall **never** hunger; and he that believeth on me shall **never** thirst." Also there is the passage from the Ephesian epistle: "To know the love of Christ which passeth knowledge, that you might be filled with all the fullness of God" (3:19). These two passages challenge us as Christians to know total deliverance and total fulfillment in our lives today. Yet, if we are really honest, most of the Christian world would have to say that this is only an aspiration which can **never** be attained right here and right now. For we mistakenly think that total deliverance and total fulfillment are only really attainable in our **future** heavenly home.

Why did Jesus promise fulfillment if it is only a carrot on a stick designed to tease us? The one thing we all know about God's nature is that "He cannot lie" (Titus 1:2). So, if Jesus promised it, then total satisfaction is available to us today. That is why Paul prays for us in the Ephesian epistle:

"That the God of our Lord Jesus Christ, the Father of glory, may give unto you the spirit of wisdom and revelation in the knowledge of him: The eyes of your understanding being enlightened; that you may know what is the hope of his call, and what the riches of the glory of his inheritance in the saints." Paul is saying that we have an inheritance in Christ that we haven't even seen let alone entered into.

What we don't realize is that there are two deliverances available to us by the Cross of Christ. We Christians understand the first deliverance from our past sins, through faith in the blood of Christ. We realize the forgiveness of our past sins, we know our future is secure, and we confidently look to heaven as our eternal home. This gives us peace from the past and assurance for the future, but what about our present tense experience? Can't we all agree that most of us live a roller coaster life of trying and failing, falling far short of what Jesus promised in John 6:35 (never thirsting, never hungering)?

What does total deliverance mean? I believe the Gospel is much deeper and broader than most Christians realize. We have heard only half of the Gospel, the provision of the precious blood. **Never** do we hear that there is deliverance in the precious **body** of Christ. I often hear Christians singing "there is power, power, wonder working power, in the blood of the Lamb," but I have never heard anyone say or sing, "there is wonder working power in the **body** of the Lamb." **But there is!**

Jesus brings out both aspects of the gospel when he makes this provocative statement in John 6:53-57; "Verily, verily, I say unto you, except you **eat** the flesh of the Son of man, and **drink** his blood, you have no life in you. Whosoever eats my flesh, and drinks my blood, has eternal life, and I will raise him up at the last day. For my flesh is meat indeed, and my blood is drink indeed. He that eats my flesh, and drinks my blood, dwells in me, and I in him. As the living Father has sent me, and **I live by** the Father; so he that **eats me, even he shall live (daily) by me**."

We know that eating and drinking are metaphors for faith. Faith is receiving what is available to us, and what we take, like food, takes and becomes us. God is satisfied when we take by faith (drink) the blood of His Son, because "without the shedding of blood there is no remission of sins." Without our receiving that provision we are still in our sins.

But why are we Christians so dissatisfied in our daily lives? I believe it is because we have never entered into the **second deliverance** provided for us by the body death and resurrection of Christ; "Except you eat my **flesh,** you will have no life **in** you." Eating His flesh means that we take the provision of His bodily death and resurrection as our present tense deliverance. The blood of Christ satisfies **God,** and the body of Christ satisfies **us**. When God and **man** are **both** satisfied, then we will never hunger or thirst again.

What are the available provisions in the "**Blood** and **Body**"of Christ? These two aspects of the gospel are symbolized in the Lord's supper: the wine and the bread. The **Blood of Christ**, symbolized by the wine, is offered to guilty and **hopeless** sinners as a provision for our sins. Jesus Christ took our sins on himself and bore the full death penalty. This sacrificial offering totally satisfied God's justice, thereby setting us free from sin. Then, by the miracle of the resurrection, Jesus was raised from the dead for our justification, thereby, giving us eternal life. The blood gives us peace with God, the forgiveness from our past sins, and security for our future destiny.

Secondly, the **Body of Christ**, symbolized by the bread, is offered to **helpless** saints as our present tense deliverance. The deeper element of the gospel is that Jesus **became** the very nature of **sin**, which is Satan expressing himself as us (II Cor. 5:21). Jesus became sin and then died to it, and in his resurrection we are made one with his righteousness. There is a **nature exchange**, thereby exchanging our consciousness from a separated striving-self-sufficient consciousness, which is the nature and mind of

Satan, to Christ's own life **as** us. Christ didn't come to improve us, He came to replace us.

The Cross (body death) exchanges sin's nature of self-centeredness with Christ's nature of "other love;" it exchanges sin's consciousness of separation with Christ's own mind of oneness; and finally, it exchanges sin's operation of striving self-effort with Christ's own operation of faith, causing us to know oneness with Christ..

Let us look deeper into the full meaning of the Body of Christ. We can begin by answering the question, "What is the Body of Christ?" The Body of Christ is his humanity or his human-ness. My good friend Linda Bunting says, "The Jews deny Jesus' divinity, while we Christians deny His humanity." We know that the Bible says that He was God in the flesh, but to most people that means an all-knowing consciousness without weakness and human limitations. Somehow, we think that weakness and humanity are sinful and wrong in themselves, therefore denying Jesus' humanity the same way we deny our own. We must look deeper into the life of Christ to know that when God became flesh, he became as weak and as capable of human frailties, emotions, and desires as we are: He truly became like us.

5.
Jesus Christ, the Human!

"Wherefore in all things in behoved Him to be made like unto His brethren, that He might be a merciful and faithful high priest"
(Hebrews 2:17).

Hebrews 5:8 says, "Jesus learned obedience by the things that He suffered." Learning is the process of evolving illumination combined with experiences. When Jesus left heaven and took on human limitation, He left his all-knowing God consciousness behind. Philippians 2:6-9 says, "Who, being in the form of God, thought it not robbery to be equal with God: But made Himself of no reputation, and took upon him the form of a servant, and was made in the likeness of man. And being found in fashion as a man, He humbled Himself, and became obedient unto death, even the death of the Cross." We may ask, "But wasn't He unlimited in his operation as the second person of the Trinity--He could walk on water and raise the dead?" Yes, God operated through Him and He was God, but He was God in human form or "in the flesh," John 1:14. God had to so identify with man, that he had to be just like us. He had to feel like we do and think like we do in order to completely know himself as a man.

As a child, Jesus grew up just like all the other Hebrew children. I think He was just as surprised as the Scribes were when He knew and understood the scriptures and spoke with great wisdom and authority in the temple at the age of twelve.

Then when He told his mother, "I am **about** my Father's business," He certainly didn't have the same confidence as his later declaration of "**I am** the way, the truth and the life." There was an evolution in the consciousness of Jesus, just as there is in ours.

I wonder about those early thirty years when he was hidden to the world. I wonder if he thought to himself, "Is carpentry all that I am going to be doing? Is this what it means to be God's son?"; or even "Am I really God's son?" I think that when he began to hear about John the Baptist, He went out to hear him in wonderment and curiosity. Probably as Jesus began to listen to John, he was pierced in his heart by the Spirit. That is why he made his way down to the place where John was baptizing. As he came into the water that day, he was humbled beyond words as his and John's spirits leaped together with recognition. Then the complete Godhead met in total agreement and confirmed Him as the beloved Son of God. He finally knew without any shadow of doubt who He really was.

Yet even the Son of God could not live on revelation alone. He had to know how He would operate as God's son **in human form**, and that meant testing. That is why the Spirit drove him into the wilderness to be tempted by Satan. He had to learn the one crucial lesson concerning his humanity. And that lesson had to be learned through suffering. Jesus learned that his humanity had no power of its own and was totally helpless in and of itself. Satan taunted him to perform, while Jesus waited in weakness for the Spirit to answer Satan's demands. "The Captain of our salvation was made perfect by the things that He suffered" (Heb. 2:10). He learned the meaning of functioning as man and God in perfect union as one, "Not by might, nor by power, but by my Spirit, saith the Lord" (Zech. 4:6). Then, after the temptations were over, his humanity was anointed by the Spirit of God, fully equipping him for his ministry. (See the chapter entitled "The Temptations of Christ.")

I find it interesting that in the Gospel of John, between chapters 4 and 14, Jesus is constantly hammering at the same point, "I can of my own self do nothing" (John 5:30). He reiterates it 36 times in one form or another through these chapters. This could have been over a period of two years. I know myself that when the Lord gives me revelation on a point, I usually repeat it everywhere I go and as often as given opportunity. Each time I say it, it gets stronger and more clear. I think that Jesus experienced the very same thing. In John 14, He was so settled in the function of his humanity that He emphatically says, "If you have seen me, you have seen the Father." He had learned that the human self had no power of its own, but was indwelt by the power of another, who was His life. The perfect nothing containing and expressing the perfect all.

As Jesus knew the secret of who he was and how he operated as a God-Man, he could share that same secret with his disciples. He first taught and foretold of the indwelling Spirit in John 14. Then in John 15 He gave them an example of functioning union relationship; "I am the vine, you are the branch; without me you can do nothing, for the branch cannot bear fruit of itself, except it abide in the vine." A branch has no life of its own, and abides by receiving its life from the vine. Jesus knew that the disciples would not understand what he meant until later, after they had received the Holy Spirit. Then He, the Holy Spirit, would reveal all things unto them.

Finally, by the time He was ready to go to the Cross, He was in great faith as He prayed for the oneness that was yet to come--first in his disciples and then in future generations; "That they all may be one; as thou, Father, art in me, and I in thee, that they also may be one in us; I in them, and thou in me, that they may be perfected in unity" (John 17:21&23). Christ paid a great price to bring this fullness to his body.

This was the evolving process that caused Jesus to know who He was and how He functioned as a man. I John 2:12-14 tells us that there is the same evolutionary process in us: **Little Children** know their sins are forgiven, **Young men** find their true identity and learn how to function as a Spirit person above Satan's assaults, while **Fathers** co-operate in the redeeming work of the Spirit according to God's eternal purposes.

Martin Luther once said: "It was God's intention to have a race of Christs. Nothing less than this is true holiness and the Gospel in operation. Holiness stands for Christ in you, the fulness of the Holy Spirit, the baptism of the Spirit and identification with Christ in His death and resurrection."

6.

The Body Death
("Dead to Sin")

"How shall we that are <u>dead to sin</u> live any longer therein?"
(Romans 6:2)

God became a human being by taking the form of His son, Jesus (John 1:14). Jesus **had** to become flesh because it takes a human to deliver the human race. Animal sacrifices could never finally deliver the human; for it is not possible that the blood of bulls and of goats should take away sins. God declares that, "sacrifice and offering thou wouldest not, but a **body** hast thou prepared me" (Hebrews 10:5-6). His human body was the sinless vessel suited for the sacrificial work of reconciliation. "To wit, that God was in Christ Jesus, reconciling the world unto himself, not imputing their trespasses unto them" (II Cor. 5:19).

The word "reconcile" means "to change from one state into another" or to exchange. What needs to be exchanged? Jesus told Nicodemus that he **must** be born-again of God's Spirit. At Nicodemus' birth he inherited a sinful spirit which had to be replaced by a holy and righteous Spirit. Without that Holy Spirit indwelling him, it was impossible for him to comprehend what Jesus was saying. He could not learn the things of God without the Holy Spirit. There had to be an exchange of spirits! The human vessel called Nicodemus wasn't the problem, it was a fallen satanic nature that caused his blindness and sinfulness. Nicodemus as well as everyone born into the world **must** have an exchange take place in their spirit's center, for only this spirit exchange can reconcile us back to God and produce in us the "new creation" (II Cor. 5:17), which is our new identity.

Through the fall, we were indwelt by a satanic-nature which caused us to commit sin. Romans 6:17 says that we were "slaves to sin," or in bondage to Mr. Sin. This sin spirit is so deep in our consciousness that it appears to be just naturally us. Ephesians 2:1-3 gives us biblical clarity on our fallen condition, "Wherein in times past ye walked according to the course of this world, according to the **prince of the power of the air**, the **spirit** that now worketh **in** the children of disobedience." This passage is saying that Satan expresses his sinful nature through us, deceiving us and making us think it **is us**.

Jesus told the Pharisees that they were "of their father the devil," because they expressed the devil's lust through them as if it **were** them (John 8:44). So in our fallen state we have inherited a satanic nature that enslaves us in our spirit's center, and causes us to sin.

Through the redemptive work of the Cross, God has provided a way for his children to be delivered from their satanic rule and brought back to himself. God sent his son Jesus to take our place on the Cross, vicariously become what we were, so that we might become what he is. "Forasmuch then as the children are partakers of flesh and blood, he (Jesus) also himself likewise took part of the same; that through death he (Jesus) might **destroy him** that had the power of death, that is, **the devil**; and deliver them (us) who through fear of death were all their lifetime subject to bondage" (Heb. 2:14-15).

Now how did God through his son Jesus accomplish this? II Cor.5:21 gives us the key. "For God hath **made** Christ, who knew no sin, **to be sin** for us, that we might be made the righteousness of God in Him." Let us begin by looking at what the Bible calls "sin." There are two grammatical uses for "sin": one is "sins" (a verb), and the other is sin (a noun). "Sins" are the action of the producer

Sin. The word "**sin**" in II Cor. 5:21 and many such verses throughout Romans is rendered a noun: The <u>Critical Lexicon and Concordance to the English and Greek New Testament</u> by Ethelbert W. Bullinger says, "Sin is not merely, however, the quality of an action, but a principle manifesting itself in the activity of the subject, the 'man of sin,' II Thes. 2:3, the personal embodiment of sin."

Therefore, "sin" is a person (Satan) expressing himself through our humanity. Then "sins" are the forms of manifestation that Sin takes, somewhat like root and fruit. If a gardener had a weed in his garden, he would not go out daily and cut off the top (sins) of the weed, he would permanently eliminate the weed by cutting it out at the root (Sin). The Cross has provided permanent deliverance to the sin problem. John the Baptist declares that Jesus, the lamb of God, takes away the **sin** (not sins) of the world" (John 1:29) and does it by laying an ax to the **root**" (Matt. 3:10). Now how did God deliver mankind?

God made the human Jesus **become sin**, because only a **perfect** vessel could contain sin and vicariously die to it for others. It is a very strong thing to say that Jesus became sin, for it means that he took on Satan. The only way for God to deliver mankind was to become what we were and die to it. For we know that in a death the spirit comes out of the body. Likewise, the spirit of Satan came out of the human Jesus who represented all humanity. Jesus' dead body was in the grave without a spirit for three days, signifying that it was completely dead. Then the Holy Spirit of God came into that dead body and raised Him from the dead, and not only Him, for we were raised with Him as well (Romans 8:11).

This truth that Paul writes, as Peter says, "is hard to understand"(II Peter 3:16), so let me reiterate: Christ died as us "made sin," expressing as us the sin nature. Therefore, in that death, out of our bodies went the false nature forever (Romans 6:6&10). Then Christ, in that risen body, representing us, raised us up with His own nature of Holiness. **Christ replaced Satan as us!** To put it simply, Jesus was joined to Mr. Sin (us) in his death, that we might be joined to Mr. Righteousness (Jesus) in his resurrection.

The blood of Christ covers the **product** of sin, which are sins; while the body death replaces the **producer** of sin. Romans 5:10 says that "For if, when we were enemies, we were reconciled to God by the **death** of his Son, much more, being reconciled, we shall be **saved by his life**." When we were hopeless sinners and enemies to God we were saved by his death, but **now** as helpless saints we shall be saved daily by his resurrected life, in us and as us.

There was a great exchange of spirits! That is why the mystery of the Gospel is "Christ in you" the only hope of glory (Col. 1:27). Now through the Cross, we are Christ in our unique human forms.

7.
Romans 7
("Dead to the Law")

"Wherefore, my brethren, ye also are become <u>dead to the law</u> by the body of Christ; that ye should be married to another, even to Him who is raised from the dead, that we should bring forth fruit unto God"
(Romans 7:4).

Since we are delivered from the old sinful nature, which is Satan in us, by the body death, then why do we still sin? This question is exactly what Paul is addressing in Romans seven. Technically, we <u>are</u> "dead to sin" by the bodily death and resurrection of Christ (Romans 6:2). Yet experientially, it doesn't seem to work too well, because there is yet one all important final lesson to learn, and it has to do with our supposed self-sufficiency. That is why Paul brings out the **second** fact that by the body death, we are also "**dead to the law**." For the outer law presupposes that we have a life of our own with the power to live and keep the law by self-effort. God must expose this lie, so he uses the law to accomplish just that.

Self-sufficient self patterns run deep in our consciousness. These false patterns were put into mankind by Satan at the fall. It is really **his** mentality. When Romans 6:6 says, "Knowing this that our old man has been crucified with him in order that the body of sin might be destroyed, that henceforth we should not serve sin," it means that the old satanic nature was put to death with Christ, releasing **my spirit** from the satanic spirit. The verse goes on to say that the full purpose of this release is to destroy "the body of sin," which is satanic self-effort expressed in **my humanity.** Don't most of us Christians say this to ourselves: "**I will** do better next time, that is, if I try harder."

The Satanic **"I will"** infected mankind at the Fall (see: "Origin of the Lie"). This infection is so deep in our consciousness that we falsely believe the human container can willfully do the works of God. "**I will** do the works of God, or **I will** be like Jesus, or even **I will** keep myself from evil." These are false lies that most Christians live by. That is why it is absolutely necessary for the Holy Spirit to expose this falsehood. We can never know the glory of being a perfect nothing until this exposure comes.

The mystery begins to unravel in Romans 6:14, "sin shall not have dominion over us because we are not under the law, but under grace." Now if we turn this verse around we will see what it is saying: Sin **shall** have dominion over you if you are **under the law**! A self that tries to keep the law (I ought to perform) by self-effort operates from a false illusionary power. I Corinthians 15:56 says, "the strength of sin is the law." The more we try, the more the law shouts at us to do more. So, trying to do good becomes the believer's greatest sin. That is very subtle, because it seems good. Yet Satan himself was not trying to be evil when he said, "I will be like the most High God" (Isa. 14:14). He was trying to be good like God. So like Paul in Romans 7:19, **trying to be good became his evil**.

Human performance based on self-sufficiency is a mentality of a satanic realm that invaded our **consciousness** through the Fall and continues to hold us in bondage as long as we live from it. There is a scripture in Hebrews 9:14 that promises us that through the Cross we will have a cleansed consciousness: "Purge (cleanse) your consciousness from dead works to serve a living God." And again in Hebrew 10:2, "Once purged we should have no more consciousness of sins."

We Christians are more "sin" conscious than "Christ" conscious. The scriptures are clear, Christians are provided a way through the Cross to be cleansed of sin, as well as from a condemned sin-consciousness, and Romans 7 shows us how.

The unknown factor in the Christian is that the human is, and always has been, the instrument of someone else. Yet in Romans 7, the one manipulating Paul is Satan. "The evil which I **would** not, that I do; Oh wretched man that I am, who will deliver me from this body of death" (Romans 7:19&24). Our problem is that we have not yet discovered the secret concerning our humanity, and the way to discover it is through the roller coaster dilemma of trying and failing.

Man has to be broken under the bondage of Satan because he must see the one simple fact that he is only a vessel. In Romans 7 Paul is being controlled by Satan, when he is actually a child of God. What opposites! Heaven and hell in the same body. I tell you it is the most radical situation any man can be in. The self is shattered into a million pieces. All the false idols of **"I can do it"** crumble. The false pride that is built on the foundation of false goodness falls on its face before the commandment of "Thou shall have no other gods before me." We must be naked and stripped of all vain ideas of self-improvement; then we will finally see our total helplessness. Before I was a Christian I had to see myself utterly hopeless without Christ, and now I have to see myself utterly helpless and weak as a born-again person. Hopeless sinners and helpless saints. Both are necessary!

Weak humanity is always and only a vessel, a simple clay pot, nothing more than a helpless container of someone else. The Christian can not really unite in oneness to her true husband, Christ, while still half way thinking she is able to do some good. The truth is that we (the human) have never been able to **produce** one ounce of good, nor one ounce of evil apart from our husband and mate. For the human (the female) is a neutral container and not the producer of her own content.

This is the greatest mystery in the universe and can only be seen by its opposite misused form first. "Unless we have plainly once for all seen our problem was Satan **not us**, and our release is Christ **not us**, we stumble along where we should be 'mounting with wings like eagles' (Isaiah 40:31) and running without weariness and walking without fainting."(Grubb, Norman; <u>The Law of Opposites</u>).

God commands Satan to do his last and final work on us Christians. This radical stripping is done at God's appointed time, for only He knows how to cleanse his created vessel. God says in Deuteronomy 32:39, "I, even I, am He, I wound, and I heal." As in Job, God says again, "Have you (Satan) considered my servant Job?" God uses his convenient agent, Satan, to do the final work of tearing down all the remnant of false sufficiency and expose the fact that self-sufficiency is not produced by us, but by Satan.

"Yet, the Cross has to be real before there can be a steady realization of the resurrection. It is a real death in experience, and probably there has to be a period when we are much more conscious of our having died with Him than having risen with Him. By no other means can we be understanding servants of Christ. We must have really tasted of the self-defeating activities of independent self in our redeemed lives and have really become soured on them. We must have come to some final point of desperation and despair to have learned our lesson with an utter finality that this way of life, of us serving Christ rather than of Him serving Himself in and by us, is a spill-over into our new lives of the great curse of the Fall, the delusion of self-sufficiency. It has to be a revelation--that the ultimate form of sin is a misuse of self, just as it then can become a personal revelation that the misuse of self is what was removed in the cross and is thus removed in us." (Grubb, Norman P. <u>God Unlimited</u>; pg. 63).

8.

"Not I, but sin"

"For I delight in the law of God after the inward man; Now then it is no more I that do it, <u>but sin</u> that dwelleth in me."
(Romans 7:22&17)

It is obvious that the Christian cannot produce good, but it is not so obvious that the Christian cannot produce evil. Most Christians would say that the good I do is Christ, but the evil I do is **my sinful flesh**. If human flesh can produce evil of itself, then the implication is that flesh can produce good of itself! That is the subtle sin of self-righteousness. That is why this lie had be exposed. Paul discovers in Romans 7:17 that the evil he did was Satan disguised as him and operating in him. Satan had his hold on him, simply because Paul was deluded to think that he was the one who <u>ought to</u> have the power, and <u>ought to</u> overcome his coveting by self-effort.

Self-righteousness and Self-effort are his hidden sins.

I would like to reenact Paul's agony in Romans 7:7-25. He opens by asking this all pervasive question, (I will paraphrase):

> What is wrong with me? I can't stop coveting other people's possessions. I'm trying like all good Christians should, but I'm not getting anywhere. Why can't I stop? What is wrong with me?

Is my problem God's law? The more I try to keep it the more I fail and end up doing the opposite. Did God give it to me just to torment me? Because the more I try to keep it, the more sinful I become. If the law wasn't there torturing me I would be much better off. Yet, I know better than that, the law is a picture of God's holiness. How can I blame God for giving us this standard?

God certainly used the law to break me in the beginning when I was first saved. It showed me how utterly hopeless and sinful I was without Christ. I consider it my best teacher. Could God be using it a second time to show me something else? Anyway, I can't blame the law, or God, for I am the one to blame, it is me that is unable to perform it. I love to keep the law, because I love to do what God wants me to do. Yes that is right, the law is not my problem for I know it is Holy, Just and Good. I am so frustrated, then what is it?

Here I am again back to me--all roads end up here with me the guilty person, full of condemnation. But let me look deeper into myself and my motives. If I'm really honest with myself, I don't want to do the things that I end up doing--I even agree with the law that I shouldn't. For I know I should not covet, but how to have the power to stop is beyond me. There is a me that does not want to sin. Oh, then I see, that <u>me</u> must be right. Well then what is it, what is wrong with me? Please God tell me.

But wait a minute! Is there something, or someone else inside me using me, or should I say, misusing me? Now, I see it is not me producing my sins. It is sin (Satan) still dwelling in my flesh members. He is deceiving me to make me think that I am the one producing sin, when it is he disguised as me. What a deceiver! All this time he was talking to me in first person. He was telling me that I should try harder, and then accusing me for not being able to do it. He is a liar, and the Father of this lie.

Now I see, the human self cannot produce sins. I knew that I couldn't produce righteousness, but I thought I could produce sins. That is why I condemned myself so much. That is a lie. If there is a possibility of me producing evil, then I have the ability to produce good. I know better than that, because that is self-righteousness. But thinking that I could do the evil is just as prideful.

This lie was set in motion because the law shouted at me to not covet, and self-sufficient-self, which is Satan, automatically operated in me trying hard not to covet. Now how can I stop trying when it is so easy? There I am again trying to stop trying. This is a real death! How do I get out of this. I'm trapped! Who can deliver me from this body of death? Oh, God please help me.

Wait a minute, "trying" is works, and I am a faith person. All I can do is leap into the person of Christ in me, and trust him to produce His righteousness as me. This "striving me," that tries so hard, died with Christ two thousand years ago. Yes, I am still alive, humanly speaking, but my life is not me living; it is Christ living in me. All I can do is live by faith and not even by my faith, but this I do by the faith of the Son of God.

As for Satan, he was defeated at the Cross and faith renders him powerless in me right now. The Cross is the power of God unto completed Salvation, and our word of faith is the powerful sword of the Spirit. My true identity is Christ as me and I no longer have a life of my own.

Now I see clearly that the one and only function of the Christian is to believe. Jesus himself said, "Of myself I can do nothing". Yet I think I tried to make myself greater than Jesus, by thinking that I could do good. What pride!

I am so thankful to my Savior for setting me free from this lie. I surrender my whole being to Him who raised me with Jesus two thousand years ago, and will now cause me to know this power of His resurrected life. I will agree with

him that I am already raised with him no matter how I look, or how long it takes to appear. In this transformation I will not lift one finger to make this happen; as a matter of fact I am going to just be myself, whatever that means. I've been so phony in my trying, that I wonder what I'm really like. It will be wonderful finding out. I can now accept myself as a right self.

To Paul, as well as us, the expectation for performance has always been the responsibility of the human self. Paul completely misunderstood how he functioned as a human receiver. He mistakenly thought that he was the producer of his own life, and **ought** to have the power to control himself. Operating in this **lie** causes us to do the very thing that we don't want to do, and traps us in the try and fail bondage of sin. This trap leaves us with an overwhelming sense of condemnation, failure, guilt and most of all self-hatred. **We end up loving the Savior and hating the human he saved**. Something is deadly wrong with this picture.

When Paul discovered it was **("**not I, **but sin")** that dwelled in him, he was finally free, because his real problem was exposed. He finally rightly understood the human I. The human self cannot produce good or **evil**, for the human I is nothing but the neutral container that holds the content of the deity. Vessels are not producers of their own life, but simple receivers of the life of another. We humans are somewhat like a computer with wonderful capacities and faculties, but like the computer, we cannot operate without a programmer. We were wrongly programmed by Satan, and now through Christ, we are rightly programmed. The Bible definition of us is: vessels, branches, temples, slaves, wives, and bodies.

The good news was that Paul was not the wretch he thought--the sin in **him** was not **him**, it was Satan. Therefore he had the authority of faith to say, "get behind me Satan." By a leap of faith, Paul went back to the Cross, and put the sin-spirit that indwelled and operated him on Jesus. For Jesus became that sin-Satan at the Cross. Then in Christ's resurrection, righteousness, which is the life of Christ, was transferred back into Paul as if it were his life. "For he hath made him to be sin for us, who knew no sin; that we might be made the righteousness of God in him" (II Cor. 5:21).

Louis Tucker, a good friend of mine, asked me one time: "How do I get Christ who is in me, to express Himself out of me?" I simply answered, "Say it is already done." Say what God says about you, not what you think, or feel, or see. Say, "I am resurrected with him, and I am whole complete lacking nothing!" DARE TO BE BOLD, AND SAY IT. Later Louis wrote in a letter, "No longer do we have to stand on Jordan's stormy banks and cast a wishful eye into Canaan's fair land. Now we can get across."

Arise My Butterfly

Break forth from the bonds which
have surrounded you,
and have protected you until this day when
I call you by my Spirit to arise and fly.
To fly with abandonment and
delight in that heavenly
realm for which you were created,
to fly in self abandonment to the delight
and saving of those around you.
For such beauty is hidden until it is my time
to call it forth. You have been transformed.
The old has passed away.
Behold all things have been made new.
He has tried you and you have come forth as gold.
So fly my golden butterfly.
Let the world see the precious gems with which
I have adorned you and shown
the world the beauty
with which none can compare.
For the beauty is none other than that
of my son, who is your life.

By: Chris Dew

9.
The Birth of a New Consciousness
(Romans 8)

"There is therefore now no condemnation to them which are in Christ Jesus, who walk not after the flesh, but after the Spirit."
(Romans 8:1)

How can words express the glory that filled Paul's heart as his spirit leaped in agreement with the Spirit of Life that was in him? The Spirit of Christ had set him free from the downward pulls of the law of sin and death which held him in bondage in his flesh. Paul, in Romans Seven, ends shouting his freedom cry, "I thank God through Jesus Christ our Lord. So then with the mind I myself serve the law of God; but with the flesh the law of sin"(7:25).

Paul finally had the discernment to see that there were two dimensions inside of him. One was the flesh dimension, which he was aware of all of his life, and the other was the Spirit dimension, which was a new reality to him. It was impossible for him to operate in both consciousness' at the same time. There had to be a severe stripping away of one reality and a radical replacement with the other. Paul says in Philippians 3:7 "I count all things but loss for the excellency of the knowledge of Christ Jesus my Lord for whom I have suffered the loss of **all things**, and do count them but **dung**, that I might win Christ." And Jesus says that "whosoever will save his life shall lose it: And whosoever will lose his life for my sake shall find it"(Matt, 16:25).

God's dealings with the Jewish nation at the Jordan River is a vivid picture of how God deals with Paul. If we can imagine the Jordan River flowing between the last few verses of Romans Seven and the first verse of Romans Eight, we will see Paul's dilemma. He is standing in the wilderness looking across the Jordan River at the promised place of rest. The obvious question arises. "Will I stay in the miserable, but comfortably familiar wilderness and not receive my inheritance, or will I leap into the risky unknown and receive what God has promised me?"

This enlightens us, as well as challenges us today. Which consciousness are we going to operate from? Here in Romans Seven, we will either remain in a needy, condemned, "I've got to fix myself" consciousness and operate in it, or we will leap into the Spirit dimension and operate by faith as "whole, complete and lacking nothing" (James 1:3). We cannot have both worlds. For "flesh and blood **cannot** inherit the kingdom of God"(I Cor. 15:50).

There is glorious freedom awaiting God's sons upon entering into the new promised land of no condemnation. Yet at the same time this is the place, I dare say, that most Christians get snagged and even stopped. We have never heard that Christ has come back inside of us releasing us from a striving self by giving us his own life of rest. The children of Israel did not enter into rest because of their unbelief. They paid a great price as an example to us. Let us honor their suffering by **learning** from their example.

God has strong warnings concerning this radical place. "Let us therefore fear, lest a promise being left us of entering into His rest, any of you should seem to come short of it" (Hebrews 4:1). "For we which have believed do enter into rest," as compared to the Israelites who could not enter in because of unbelief. Here in Romans 8, we reach the Jordan River in our consciousness and the penetrating question arises, do we believe what God says to be the truth, or do we believe what appears (feeling and thinking level) to be the truth? The Israelites grieved the Holy Spirit because they erred in their "evil hearts of unbelief" (Hebrews 3:7-19).

Strong language isn't it, yet this is a very serious matter, for we are standing between the bondage of a hellish me, and the freedom of a new me as Christ. Behind us is the Romans Seven desert of striving self which is death, yet before us lies the apparent impossibility of unconquerable giants. How is it possible for me to totally inherit the rest that is promised, when my soul seems so manic one minute and the next minute plummets downward to the depths of despair? My heart is comforted by the scripture knowledge that this Spiritual warfare is normal. Our Lord himself experienced satanic attacks in the wilderness. The Hebrews letter says in 10:32, "after you were illuminated, you endured a great fight of afflictions." And in 4:11, "we are to **labor** to enter into His rest." This fight and this labor is the simple leap of faith. Yet all hell tells you it is not true.

That is why Romans Eight puts great emphasis on walking in the Spirit and not in the flesh. For we have no condemnation if we **"walk not after the flesh, but after the Spirit."** If Paul walks in who he is in Christ, he has no condemnation, but if he strives to become something by self-effort, he is condemned and under the law.

Walking in the flesh is temporarily revisiting Romans Seven by falling into the trap of believing I "should," I "ought" to try to somehow improve myself, defend myself, or keep myself from evil. The illusionary "I" has reappeared and this "I" is subject to the outer law that it cannot keep. We are always being tempted downward with assaults that pull us back to self-effort: "be more patient, don't lose your temper, get rid of your evil thoughts, struggle against your lust, solve yourself, and try to fix others." "**I am a needy self so I have to DO, DO, DO in order to save myself.**" This is a lie!

Because I am so used to taking charge of my own life and trying to control myself, I easily slip back into the try and fail dilemma of Romans Seven. God puts us through **a painful process of learning how to walk in the Spirit**. The way to walk in the Spirit is always by **faith**. That means we always go back to what the **truth** is about us: since the same Spirit that raised Jesus from the grave dwells in you, **He**, the Holy Spirit, will quicken your mortal flesh! For you are not really a flesh being, **you are a Spirit being** (Romans 8: 9-11). Flesh doesn't master flesh, but Spirit masters flesh. Someone once said that we all think "we were human beings on a spiritual journey, but in fact we are really Spirit beings on a human journey."

The truth is that the law of Spirit and Life which is Christ as us, **has set us free** from the law of sin and death (Satan's bondage in our flesh level). It is already done. For what we could not do for ourselves, Christ did by "condemning sin in our flesh" (Rom. 8:3), thereby freeing us to be joined to our true husband, Christ, who fulfills the "righteousness of the law in us"(8:4).

The Cross defeated the whole satanic reign in our flesh by condemning Satan and putting him behind prison bars, thereby rendering him **powerless**. Satan is bound but not gagged, for he can still shout accusations at us behind prison bars, which he does constantly (Rev.12:10). This is why we have to learn how to walk in the Spirit truth and not in Satan's accusing lies.

We must learn **not** to look at what is seen, for Satan would have us look down at our flesh appearance, which is "the mind set on the flesh." If we do, God promises us that **we will die** (8:6a). But if we dare look at the unseen and fix our gaze there, we are setting our "minds on the Spirit." That mind-set promises us life and peace (8:6b). Let us shout the victory before it comes into outer manifestation. We can now claim our right **not** to be condemned, we will not receive that lie anymore. However we appear, there is "**now** (present tense) **no-condemnation.**"

We fight by **not** fighting, just like Jehoshaphat the king, "**Ye shall not need to fight** in this battle; set yourself, stand ye still, and see the salvation of the Lord "(II Chron. 20:17). Now the onus is on God, for we cannot stop ourselves from striving. **God** is the one that causes our faith stand to appear in our flesh. However, we are not going to watch for it to happen, for that would be "the mind set on the flesh" again. As far as we are concerned, we are going to **accept ourselves** as right selves, "whole, complete and lacking nothing." That is the "mind set on the Spirit."

God promises us that if we "walk in the Spirit we **shall not** fulfill the lust of the flesh"(Gal. 5:24). How do we walk in the Spirit? We just "be" ourselves and expect the Spirit to **cause** us to walk in God's ways, "and do them." "I will put my Spirit within you, and **cause** you to walk in my statutes, and you shall keep my judgments, and do them" **(Ezek. 36:26-27)**.

The Gospel is an exchange of gods, not an exchange of flesh. There was not one thing wrong with Paul's flesh, in fact, there never was. Christ won the victory over Satan in Paul's humanity, at the Cross (Romans 6:6). Therefore the fight is over. **We can now leap into the person of Christ as our Victor, and our Rescuer, and our Life**. We cease from trying to be our own savior and cannot touch our rescue. We confess with God that it is "not by (our) power, or by (our) might, but by my Spirit saith the Lord"(Zech. 4:6). When you know the truth and agree with God, the lie falls away because it looses its false power. "You shall know the truth and the truth shall set you free"(John 8:32).

This operation is the total work of the Holy Spirit as He births our consciousness from self-loathing to self-love and self-acceptance, from self-effort to Spirit believing. We cannot touch this process. It is a metamorphosis, somewhat like a butterfly coming out of its cocoon. There is a transformation taking place inside of us as all the false realities die in the brightness of Christ, "the day star," rising in us, as us. Like the butterfly, we shed our grave clothes of false belief in a false self. Every lie drops off with the cocoon in the glory of His coming.

When this happens we do not lose our unique human self with all its faculties and capacities. The grave clothes are not our humanity, but the lies we've believed about our humanity. We were never wrong, we were indwelt by a false god, who misused our precious humanity. What we do lose is the illusion of an independent self we believed in. What we gain is the glory of Christ's Spirit and my spirit, merges together as **one spirit being.** It is an interpenetrating of spirits. So much so, that we don't know where one stops and the other begins.

Most Christians can say that Christ lives **in** them, but confessing that Christ is **as us** is another story. My friend Linda once said that, saying Christ is as us, is **"the ultimate form of loving ourselves."** We have to take a leap of faith to say it, for it doesn't seem to be the truth. But until we do take a leap and say, **"Christ as us,"** then we are not accepting the form that Christ is taking as us, and ultimately we are not believing God, for Ephesians 1:5 says: He has "predestined us unto the adoption of children by Jesus Christ to himself, according to the good pleasure of His will to the praise of the glory of His grace, wherein He has **made us accepted** in the beloved." God has accepted us, therefore, we by faith, accept ourselves.

Saying the truth will cause us to suffer though, because on the appearance level it seems untrue. Paul suffered to fully know who he was. We too, will suffer, just like the butterfly suffers as it emerges to its glory. This suffering is the one condition of our being sons. "You are a co-heir if so be that you suffer with him" (Romans 8:17). The perfect God-man, Jesus Christ, was forced into perfection through the things He suffered (Hebrews 2:10). So it is fitting that we also learn the obedience of faith by the things we suffer.

Through all of this metamorphosis, all we have is our word of faith, for all God has is His **Word**. In fact His **Word** framed the worlds (Hebrew 11:2). Jesus is called the **Word**.

We are sanctified through "the **Word** of truth" (John 17:17). Jesus told the centurion he had great faith when he asked Jesus to heal his servant by speaking the **word only** (Matthew 8:8). Jesus also said, "by your **words** you shall be justified and by your **words** you shall be condemned" (Matthew 12:37). And finally, Revelation 12 speaks of that great war in heaven when Satan, the deceiver of the whole world, is cast out. How did the saints overcome him? By the blood of the Lamb, and by the **word** of their testimony, for they loved not their lives unto death. The saints overcame Satan because they put their faith in the finished work of the Cross and stood on their word of faith alone.

This is the declaration of emancipation of the human self! It is revolutionary! All hell screams at us as if we are liars. We fight by **not** fighting, and by leaping into the person of Christ who is our rest. Satan is the liar and the father of illusions, but we don't judge by appearances, but judge righteous judgment and walk by faith.

Faith is substance, and the substance is within us supernaturally. Faith is not built on reason, it is built on fact. The fact is that we are complete in Christ, lacking nothing (Colosians 2:9-10). All we have is our word of faith, yet the strength doesn't come from our word. The strength comes from Christ, the one we are putting our faith in. Our word might be very weak, even seeming as small as a mustard seed. But wasn't Abraham's faith small in the beginning? He could only hope when everything looked hopeless (Romans 4:18). We must take heart, for is anything too hard for God?

Second Corinthians 3:18 shows us how to be transformed by the Spirit. It begins in verse 17 by saying, "The Lord is that Spirit; and where the Spirit of the Lord is there is liberty." This verse is saying that the Holy Spirit will do the work. This frees us from trying to sanctify ourselves. Then it goes on to say in verse 18, "But we all, with open face beholding as in a glass the glory of the Lord, are changed into the same image: from glory to glory, even as **by** the Spirit of the Lord" (II Cor. 3:17-18).

Our only part in this whole process is to just look into a mirror. The question is; do I just see myself alone? Or do I dare to see, by faith, the glory of the Lord in my human form? By simply gazing into the mirror of my true identity, I am changed from glory to glory even by the Spirit of the Lord.

It seems simple, but hell screams at you, telling you the very opposite. That is why the Psalmist says, "He prepares you a table, in the presence of your enemies." God's table is full, filled with the heavenly food of truth, but you must eat it at the accusing finger of our enemy. He does this purposely, for it is His way of fixing us. Opposition forces us to say the truth. If we don't, we die under the weight of hopelessness. Yet even when we are so weak that it seems impossible to say the truth, we can depend on his word in II Tim. 2:13, "If we believe not, yet He abideth faithful; He cannot deny Himself." The glory of the Lord finally comes into being as God "anoints my head with oil, my cup runneth over; Surely goodness and mercy shall follow me all the days of my life, and I will dwell in the house of the Lord forever" (Psalm 23:5&6).

My husband, Scott, said something interesting the other day about faith. He said, "Faith takes too long for most people, so we have to devise ways to help God get rid of our evils." In a day of micro-wave living with instant everything, we think we need instant answers. But James says, "let patience have her perfect work that you may be perfect and entire, lacking nothing." So actually it is in not seeing that we really learn faith.

Faith does dissolve into knowing however. For faith becomes a settled fact in us, more sure than our outer reality. That is why Jesus said to Peter, "Upon this rock I will build my church, and the gates of hell cannot prevail against it." Inner revelation knowing is unmovable. For what we take by faith becomes a living reality in us.

This process of faith is a miracle. Christ becomes the new free and spontaneous you. You will not be able to explain how it happens because this new life comes from the other side (the Spirit). One day you will look back at your past and wonder what happened to the you who hated yourself so much. As you rise, the old falls away and death has no sting, because you have no more fight. Finally you are then free to love and accept yourself.

God must expose Satan by bringing him to the **foreground** in Romans 7. Then after Satan's exposure and defeat in us, he is hardly noticeable in the **background,** for he is finally put under the feet of Jesus (Hebrews 10:13). Our consciousness is changed from a divided sin-and-devil consciousness to a unified seeing of God only. We never again see Satan as an enemy to be feared. We have overcome him by the blood of the Lamb and the word of our testimony (Rev. 12:11). Now, we are as Paul says in Romans 16:19, "simple towards evil," because we see how it fits back into God's purposes.

We walk on the unseen waters of the truth. The miracle is that what we take must take us, and comes back as an echo inside our consciousness as a confirming witness (I John 5:10). That is when we cry as Paul did in Romans 8, "Abba, Father." The son has possessed his possessions and comes home to the Father within. Job's hopeful cry, "Yet in my flesh shall I see God," races through time and bursts into manifestation in us today.

Paul's divided consciousness is finally united into the oneness of the mind of Christ. For it is Christ's own mind manifesting in Paul's mind. Paul can now begin to see that "the sufferings of this present world" are not worthy of comparison "with the glory that is revealed in us"(8:18). Even at the fall, we were subjected to suffering and "vanity, not willingly, but by reason of Him, who hath subjected the same in hope"(8:20). None of us wanted suffering, but now we can see that God subjected us to it, because the only way we can know God's grace and glory is in comparison to our sin and suffering.

Even in Paul's new resurrected life he has suffering. For agony is right, and the opposite end of the authority of faith. Now he **is a trustworthy son. For he has gotten**

himself back as a right self. God can trust him with the intercessions of others Even our groaning and weaknesses are right and part of the price we all pay as intercessors. We travail and "groan within ourselves with groaning that cannot be uttered." In our weaknesses' we don't even know how to pray, but the Spirit helps our infirmities (8:26-27).

The glory of it all is "that **all things** work together for good to them that love God, to them who are called according to his purposes." **All** means everything, good or evil, working together as God's perfect plan to conform us to the image of His Son" (8:28-29).

Finally, Paul ends this chapter by recognizing that he has inherited the very nature of God, which is totally self-giving. His attitude is spontaneously Christ-like. "For thy sake we are killed all the day long; we are accounted as sheep for the slaughter. Nay, in all these things we are more than conquerors through him that loved us" (8:36-37). Paul's concern is instantly for others and how God's redemptive purposes will be fulfilled through him. Whatever the cost, Paul's life is for others. If it means peril, tribulation, famine, the sword, or even death, it matters not. For **nothing** can separate him from God and His love for him. Christ has come back again in Paul to lay his life down for others.

Paul leaves us in Romans Eight in victorious union with Christ, and with sufficiency in all things, no matter what trials our lives might bring. His consciousness changes from a double minded, unstable mind set, to a steady single eye of seeing God only.

So now we have a total Christ in a total and complete human being. As Paul says, "So, Christ was once offered to bear the sins of many; and unto them that look for him shall he appear the second time (as us) without sin unto completed salvation." Hallelujah, what a Savior!

Gethsemane

In golden youth when seems the earth a summer-land of singing mirth, when souls are glad and hearts are light, and not a shadow lurks in sight. We do not know it, but there lies somewhere veiled under evening skies, a garden which we all must see, "The garden of Gethsemane." With joyous steps we go our ways, love lends a halo to our days; light sorrows sail like clouds afar, we laugh, and say how strong we are. we hurry on; and hurrying, go close to the border-land of woe, that waits for you, and waits for me-- Forever waits Gethsemane.

Down shadowy lanes, across strange streams, bridged over by our broken dreams; behind the misty caps of years, beyond the great salt fount of tears, the garden lies. Strive as you may, you cannot miss it in your way. All paths that have been, or shall be, pass somewhere through Gethsemane.

All those who journey, soon or late, must pass within the garden's gate; must kneel alone in darkness there. And battle with some fierce despair. God pity those who cannot say,"Not mine but thine," who only pray,"let this cup pass," and cannot see The purpose in Gethsemane.

by: Ella Wheeler Wilcox---1889

10.

A Severe Mercy
(My own treasured darkness)

"I will go before thee, and make the crooked places straight: I will break in pieces the gates of brass and cut in sunder the bars of iron: And I will give thee <u>the treasures of darkness,</u> and hidden riches of secret places, that <u>you</u> mayest know that I, the Lord, which call thee by thy name, am the God of Israel."
Isaiah 45:2-3

    I used to picture myself like a twisted ball of yarn, knotted, tangled, and rolled real tight. I always wanted to be free, but my fears caused me to hold tight to the only life I knew. All the knots of my life were painfully but gently untangled with love, and laid at my Master's feet. Only my Creator, the one who made me, could heal such a tangled mess and recreate a new me.
    Only God could break the bars of iron that held me fast. Yet, it is in darkness that the Master does his best work. That is why I love these verses of promise in Isaiah 45:2-3, "I will go before you, and make the crooked places straight: I will break in pieces the gates of brass, and cut in sunder the bars of iron: And I will give you **the treasures of darkness,** and hidden riches of secret places, that **you** may know that I, the Lord, which call you by **your name**, am the God of Israel."
    Darkness has become my best friend, for it stripped me and caused me to be humble and weak. Then my Jesus could make everything about me all right. And being made all right by

Jesus is the sweetest, most refreshing resting place in the universe.

I have not always known that I was all right, though. For some of my earliest recollections are that of dislike of myself. As a child I hated myself; I always thought I was dumb and a terrible misfit. In reality I had a learning disability which is dyslexia. But my misconceptions of myself probably account for my low self-esteem and a lot of why I thought I was such a stupid misfit.

As a child, I tried to read my school lessons to my mother, but because I couldn't read very well, she would slap me and tell me how dumb I was. In those days, my mother, herself, also lived in self-hatred which, of course, breeds itself. Self-hatred is so insidious. What we hate about ourselves we take out on others. Most of my childhood was spent listening to my mother preach at me. Somehow, everything I did was wrong, and that made me hate her. Yet hating her made me feel guilty. The horror of it all was that it left me feeling worthless, dumb, rejected, and very fearful.

As a teen I fought constantly with my mother and promised myself that I would never be like her. Ironically, years later I would only hope to be exactly like her. But in those days all I could do was dream of leaving home. At sixteen I ran away from home and got married to the first boy that came along. That was a total disaster because I returned home after just three months, deserted by my husband, and pregnant. This compounded my hell. Not only did I have my mother telling me what a horrible person I was, I was now telling myself as well. Failure and rejection flooded my agonizing soul. Yet, what can anyone do in that state of spiritual ignorance, except just try to cope.

Somehow I finished high school, suffering the disgrace of being without a husband, and had my baby alone at only 17. In that day and time it was very disgraceful to be divorced and raising a child, especially at my young age. It says of Jesus in Isaiah 53:3 that he was, "despised and rejected of men; a man of sorrows, and acquainted with grief." Jesus was sinless, and I was a sinner, yet he had the same feelings of rejection that I had.

That comforts me to know that my Savior knew the same sufferings that I knew.

My only solace was to go to school and try to get the best education I could. So I started into training as an X-ray technician. During the second year of my two year course, I started dating my present husband, Scott. Mom insisted on breaking us up, which eventually forced us together. When she found out that I was as adamant as she was, she threw me out of the house again. As I was leaving I grabbed my son, David. She was not going to have him. This infuriated her, for by then, she had grown very attached to him and considered David her own.

Scott took us to his stepmother's house. It was there that my first husband (paid by my parents to kidnap David) picked him up on a "visit." It was several hours later I found out that they had taken him out of town. I was devastated.

My parents were planning to try to get David from me by trying to prove that I was an unfit mother. Finally, the tension broke when my Dad came to me in tears, deciding that he could not do such a thing. They gave my baby back to me. Now I was finally away from my nemesis. Or was I? If we don't resolve our problems in God, then we can't leave them behind. They will reappear in other forms, because the only real problem we have is our own unbelief.

Scott and I got married soon after that. We had fallen in love and I dreamed of happiness and fulfillment through marriage to him. My friend Harriet calls it the "Cinderella Syndrome." I was determined to make this marriage work, no matter what it took. I was not ever going back to my mother's house to live with her again. It wasn't long into my marriage when my dreams got dashed because my prince charming was not fitting into my ideal of happiness.

Eight years of marriage and two children later, I was failing miserably again. We never run away from our problems, because our real problems are inside of us. My insecurities and fears of another divorce drove me to seek and find refuge in Christ. Although I believe that I was saved at a Billy Graham Crusade at 18, I never knew that Christ lived in me until I was again in despair at the age of 28. At that time, I was having my third child in the hospital when I met Linda Bunting, who led me to know that Christ was living his life in me. Knowing Christ filled my empty life and heart with a long awaited peace.

As soon as I could, I made my way to my mother's house to share Christ with her. I can remember standing in her kitchen telling her that if she didn't have Jesus in her life, she was going to hell. (You know, I always wanted to tell her to go to hell, but I didn't expect it to be this way.) My zealous approach was somewhat overwhelming to her, so she threw me out of her house once more.

For three days she paced the floor as she built her case against me, not knowing she was really fighting God. "How could Sylvia say such a thing to me, she must be crazy, I'm a good person." After three days of being under strong conviction by the Spirit, my mother went to her basement to iron some clothes. As she ironed, she warred away with the Spirit.

Suddenly she felt and knew the presence of the Lord. The Lord said to her, "Everything that Sylvia said is true, you **are** going to hell without me, you are already there." That instant she fell to her knees by her ironing board repenting, and received Christ. Miracles of all miracles, my mother was gloriously born-again. My Dad's conversion soon followed. Immediately she called me by phone to share her experience. Our hearts touched each other in love for the first time in our lives. This was only the beginning of God's restoring us to each other. He promises restoration, "I will restore to you the years that the locust hath eaten, the cankerworm, and the caterpillar, **my** great army which **I sent** among you" (Joel 2:25).

My mother's conversion was wonderful, but it didn't cure my insecurities about myself or my resentments towards her. I still carried them deep inside like grave clothes from the past. Finally, I reasoned with the Lord, "If **she** would apologize to me now that she is saved, maybe then I would feel more secure about myself." What self-righteousness! I didn't want to look at my part in our hellish relationship. That conveniently left me off the hook. But of course, the Lord wouldn't let me get away with that.

Finally one day the Lord said to me, "**Why does she have to apologize for what I call perfect? I dug those holes of insecurities and fears in you, so that I might fill them up with Myself Then you will really know me and the power of my resurrected life in you.**" I wrestled with the Lord; "You mean that you meant all this hell in my life? It was really you who dug these deep scars of fear and self-hatred, and all that was a form of your perfect love for me?" Suddenly I remembered the story of Joseph in the Bible. He too was treated cruelly by his brothers, yet in the end he said to them, "you meant it for evil against me, but God **meant** it for good" (Gen. 50:20). The word **"meant"** is strong. It doesn't say *permitted* it for good, but "meant it for good."

The truth is that my whole life had been designed by God. All my scars and my hells were what He meant for me as my perfect past and necessary background for seeing the truth and knowing **him as my total fulfillment**. Psalms 139:8&13 says, "You did form my inward parts, you did knit me together in my mother's womb." "If I ascend up into Heaven, you are there; if I make my bed in hell, behold, you are there."

Sometimes I think if I had gone to a psychologist at that point, I would have gone crazy trying to analyze myself and my situation. Yes, I certainly was a victim and imprisoned by my own self-hatred and self-pity, but so was my mother. She also had a horrible past, and she was also victimized. If God had not stopped the chain of sin in our family, I would have treated my children the same way that she did. Her cruel treatment of us children was only a reflection of her own self-hatred and bondage. I thank God for his word to me that day; without it I would still be blaming her and hating myself. The truth is clear and simple when you hear it from God, and it instantly heals.

I simply agreed with God that day. "You, Father meant it all for my good." Flesh reason couldn't tell me that, but the Spirit's wisdom could. I would still be in the desert of psychoanalyzing if I had not found out the Spirit's truth. It didn't come easy for me to say though, because I had to die in order to say it. I couldn't feel sorry for myself anymore, or blame my mother for my misery. I think that people get their whole identities from being victims, which I call **"the victim complex."** I know I did. Perverted as it was, I loved being the one who got hurt, because it supported my self-righteousness by making someone else the problem instead of me. Self-pity became who I was. I could hide my own sins there under my hurt feelings while I pointed an accusing finger at my mother. It's insidious because I didn't look like the bad person, I was the poor victim. She was the one who looked bad, and a part of me loved that she looked that way. But in truth, my self-pity and judgmental attitude about her was just as sinful.

A miracle happened to me that day, for God changed my heart towards my mother. I really loved her and forgave her, which of all things, healed me. Immediately she changed towards me. I have since wondered who changed first, me or her? Or was it my perspective that changed? Somehow I think my new seeing transformed me as well as her. I have seen since that we hold people in their bondage, and are in bondage ourselves because we won't forgive others.

Christ transformed her self-hatred into self-love. Then from there it grew into love for other people. I will never forget her saying, "God loves **me**!" It sounds simple and elementary, but it certainly transformed her. She became the most positive, affirming person that I ever knew. So much so that she would never let me say a condemning word about myself. What a turn-around! Needless to say, we became very best friends. She will never die in my heart because we truly have each other forever.

(The rest of my mother's story is told in the chapter entitled, "The Fellowship of His Sufferings.")

The Spirit cleared me with my mother, but what about my insecurities and fears? Did they instantly disappear? No! I subconsciously operated in this false identity as if it were the truth. "Who is Sylvia Pearce? Well, she is a fearful, insecure, condemned person who is struggling and trying to improve herself." How was I going to get rid of me? The task was too big. I couldn't blame my mother anymore, now was I going to blame myself? Forgiving my mother and seeing her rightly, still didn't solve the big **me** problem. It didn't put **me** right with **me**. Spiritually, I was seeing that I had Christ as my Savior and He was living in me, but I had Christ and a **me**, and the "me" part was desperately failing again.

My first love and peace at conversion satisfied me for a while, but it wasn't enough to make me completely satisfied with myself. My jealousies and fears of losing my husband started to overwhelm me again. I tried to hide them, but they had a way of creeping out, and it was escalating. My first thought was that I ought to be able to control myself; I shouldn't act that way. I would agree, yet the more I tried to conquer myself, the worse I got. I got sicker and sicker as the weeks went by. Finally I became a recluse, hiding away in my bedroom as much as I could.

How could I face my Christian friends? I was an embarrassment to myself and surely to them. Here I was a Bible teacher and counselor, yet I was a total mess at home with my husband and family. All I could do was hide.

My imagination was so wild that I dreamed up scenarios that were pure vanity. When I would face Scott with these false accusations, he would blow up and accuse me of being crazy. Then I would hate myself for being crazy. Around and around I went in the hell of trying to control myself and failing, only to end up back again in self-loathing. The one way God proves to us that we have **never** been in control of ourselves is to let us experience being out-of-control.

I tried confessing my sins, which I did constantly. I begged God to take them away, but nothing helped. God wouldn't take away my insanity just because I confessed sin. My whole identity was based on a lie, and that was my real root problem. God's mercy was bringing it all out into the obvious, for that lie was hidden deep in my consciousness. Painful as it was, I had to see it for what it was, so that I could finally be set free.

My madness soon led me to total depression. In desperation I found myself in my closet beating my head on the wall, screaming, "Please God, let me die, just let me die." I cried for hours. Then suddenly, the gentle voice of the Holy Spirit broke His silence and spoke into my parched consciousness. **"You are already dead!"** **"Dead?** I thought" The Spirit then asked me a question, **"What can a dead person do?"** Oh, now I see what God is after. "Nothing, I answered, a dead person can do nothing! A dead person has no life. A dead person has no power to control himself, nothing to improve about himself, and no life of his own." There was a great hesitation, then the Lord said, "Now, **I am the real you**." Through the deliverance won for me two thousand years ago at the Cross, I was crucified with him, and I (the self I hated) no longer lived, but Christ lived as me (Galatians 2:20).

I had identified myself with a self which was failing, out of control, wretched and miserable. God was now making me identify myself by his measuring stick, not mine. God sees me in union with Christ; perfect, whole, and complete (Colossians 1:22). Now I could begin to see myself as having that same new identity (Christ as me).

My problem was not that I was tempted to imagine vain things, my problem was that I wrongly thought I should have the power to conquer my thoughts and feelings. My trying by self-effort to conquer and control myself was my real sin. **The patterns of self-sufficiency and self-effort run deep in our consciousness, so deep that it takes a great blow to our egos to prove to us that we humans are nothing but common vessels.** I falsely thought that I was the one who should do good. That is a lie. The human Sylvia has no power to produce good, or evil. That power comes from what is in the vessel, and not the vessel itself.

It was good news that came to me in my closet that day, for I finally heard with my Spiritual ears and saw with my Spiritual eyes. The one and only function of the human is simply to believe, to simply agree with God. God says that I am dead and another lives my life (Colosians 3:3-4), so I **must** say it. I hardly believed it, but I obeyed God and said it anyway.

I am always getting a new interpretation as I correlate my dark time with Paul's Romans 7 experience. There is no such thing as human resource or human-performance. I did not have the power to raise myself from death, but I could speak the word of faith--I could say with God, "Christ is my deliverance, my rescue, and the real me." Light flooded my soul that day, yet I had to learn how to <u>Practice of the Presence of God</u>, as Brother Lawrence entitled his book. God forced me daily to speak to my darkness, and say the opposite. It is what Paul said about Abraham in Romans 4:17, "He calls the things that be not, as though they are." God called him his friend, because Abraham operated just like God himself operates, "Who commanded the light to come **out of** darkness" (II Cor. 4:6) at creation.

There was a period of time when I looked like I had a split personality. I remember one day when I was walking with Scott and screaming accusations at him. I stopped mid sentence and said, "This is not me, I am really Christ, and Christ isn't a crazy person, so I'm not either." Ten minutes later I was back screaming at him again. It's a wonder that he didn't divorce me; thank God for His keeping power. It is far greater than we know.

The miracle of faith is that what you take by faith, takes you. Just as when we study to learn a profession, then, one day, the profession turns around, takes us and becomes our consciousness: we don't say "I have learned to be a doctor," we say, "I *am* a doctor". What we take, takes us. All we do is affirm the truth and God confirms it inside us.

As I took the truth by faith, my insecurities and fears fell away. A new person emerged. A person that I amazingly loved, and could trust, and really appreciate. It's funny though, I hardly noticed when it all happened. All I did was just walk in faith, and refuse to look at my flesh appearances.

A new sense of self-acceptance arose in my consciousness. I even began to accept my negative reactions as right, and not try to get out of them. I started to see that my humanity was right, even such flesh reactions as jealousies, angers, and tempers. I thought to myself one day, "God is jealous isn't He? God has a temper doesn't He? God hates and He gets angry, doesn't He?" There is a right use to all these strong desires.

Galatians 5:25 says, "They that are Christ's **have crucified the flesh with the affections and lust,**" and Colossians 2:11 says, "You are circumcised with the circumcision made without hands, **in putting off the body of**

sins of the flesh by the circumcision of Christ. This simply means that at the Cross of Christ the wrong use of our flesh, which was Satan in our members, was done away with. And by faith, we can believe the truth about ourselves and dare to accept ourselves. **What God calls clean, we cannot call unclean, that is calling God a liar.**

I began to see that my flesh was rightly used by the Spirit. By the miracle of the resurrected Christ as me, the Spirit transmuted my flesh into right-Spirit-use, which is true righteousness or (right-use-ness).

Now my flesh tendencies are redirected. I am no longer coming from my need for fulfillment, because I know my own wholeness. So now my weaknesses, and jealousies are directed towards the needs of other. My weaknesses, are a signal to me that the Spirit is up to something. Most of the time, God uses my reactions as an attention getter. I often think, "God, what are you up to in this situation--what can I believe for them?"

All the things that I hated about myself and considered my liabilities are really my greatest assets. Miraculously, my attitudes change from, "What is wrong with me?" to "What is right with me?"

Soren Kierkegaard once said, "Life can only be understood backwards, but must be lived forwards." In retrospect, I can see that I am not the same person that I used to be at all. I do not hate myself, I can truly say that I love and accept myself, and in loving myself, I can love and accept others. That is a miracle!

I am forever grateful to my Father who put me through such darkness and agony. Now how can I be grateful for darkness and depression? I can, because I know it was God's mercy, His **"Severe Mercy."** Only God could love me enough to **"make** me to lie down in green pastures." For it was through failing to overcome myself, that I learned my greatest lessons.

Jesus said, "Whosoever shall loose his life, will find it" (Matt. 16:25b). In loosing my life of self-hatred, striving and misery, I could finally find my real life. I am thankful to loose the **lies** I lived by most of my life, and replace them with the truth of who I really am. "Thank you Father for giving me, back to me."

11.
Origin of the Lie

Lucifer said: "I will ascend above the heights of the clouds; I will be like the most High God."
(Isaiah 14:14)

The lie originated in Lucifer before the creation of man. Lucifer was created to be the "son of the morning, anointed cherub that covereth, sealing up the sum, full of wisdom, and perfect in beauty" (Ezekiel 28:14-18). He was created by God with the capacity to utilize and express all of the power of God's eternal glory. And he did so until iniquity was found in him, for he said in his heart, **"I will be like the Most High God,"** or "I will not be dependent on any; instead I will be a total independent-self, just like the Most High God." In doing so, his heart choice brought into being Satan, a counterfeit god. Webster defines counterfeit: "a fraudulent copy whose purpose is to deceive. This counterfeit also takes on or presents a false or deceptive appearance." Interesting isn't it? Revelation 12:9 gives us in just one verse all of the Biblical names for Satan. "And the great Dragon was cast out, that old Serpent, called the Devil, and Satan, which deceiveth the whole world: he was cast out into the earth, and his angels were cast out with him."

The creature Satan, like all of creation, is created to contain and express the life of God. But here the creature makes a deadly spirit choice, **"I WILL."** Imagine the pride in the creature saying," I have a will and life separate from God's and I will have it." This is the first and original sin. Now, not only did Satan think that he had a separate will of his own, but he then said, "**I WILL BE LIKE**." If I say to myself that I am going to be like Billy Graham, for instance, I would have to not only try, but strive hard to do it. My best efforts to imitate him would only make me a counterfeit with a deceptive appearance. Satan poses himself to be like God when in fact he is a liar, deceiver, and a mirror image counterfeit. It is interesting to me, though, that Satan wasn't trying to be evil, he was and is trying be good like God, but in doing so, he became a devil. That reminds me of Paul in Romans 7:21 "When I would do good, evil is present with me."

Satan was enamored with his own beauty, wisdom and form--his outer manifestation. He deceived himself into believing that his created form was God. Satan exchanged the truth for a lie and worshipped his created form instead of the Creator (Romans 1:25). Isn't it interesting that God says, "I am," while Satan says, "I will be like." It takes no effort to be, yet it takes lots of effort to be **like** someone! Thus the differences between **being\trusting** and **doing\self-effort**.

Satan imagined that he was an independent god with independent powers of his own. He used all his God-given capacities to exalt his throne over the stars of God and imitate the Most High. He reversed the self-giving power of God into a powerful dark self-for-self kingdom, falsely believing himself to be an independent power. But what he didn't know was that God is the only true independent one. As a result, Satan fell from his exalted position with a third of the angelic realm. Deceived as he is, he fails to see that he is really God's servant-fool, necessary opposite, and convenient agent, for nothing can be separated from the one almighty God in the universe. Paul preached that message to the unsaved Athenians when he said "in him we live, and move, and have our being" (Acts 17:28).

And then our former father the devil, at the Fall, cleverly imparted to us his self-sufficient, self-active consciousness. This made us believe in ourselves and produced a false identity. This consciousness is so much in us that it dwells in our sub-consciousness level. Consequently, we naturally operate as self-sufficient beings, even after we are Christians. Can't we all remember thinking to ourselves that we loved Jesus so much that we wanted to serve Him any way we could? Little do we know at that immature stage that even trying to be like Jesus is really an independent-self operating as if we had the power in our humanity to please God. This lie has permeated our consciousness through the fall, and is the biggest lie in the universe.

Paul gives us a clear picture in Ephesians 2:2-3 of the fallen condition of the human race. He declares, "Wherein in time past you walked according to the course of this world, according to the prince of the power of the air, the spirit that now worketh in the children of disobedience: Among whom also we all had our conversation in times past in the lust of our flesh and of the mind; and were by nature the children of wrath, even as others." Satan's self-for-self nature works in us causing us to see ourselves falsely as self-empowered independent beings.

Satan's fall was fixed in his spirit because he wanted to replace God. Adam did not want to replace God, he just wanted it **his** way. He wanted God, and his way too, which, of course, makes it sin. But his divided choice leaves room for redemption, while Satan's choice is final.

12.
Temptations of Jesus

"Then was Jesus led up of the Spirit into the wilderness to be tempted of the devil."
(Matthew 4:1)

Jesus was <u>confirmed</u> as the **Son of God** at the Jordan River and <u>settled</u> as the **son of man** by his temptation experiences in the wilderness. The son of man, as he is most often called in the Bible, learned the obedience of faith by the things that he **suffered**, Hebrews 5:8. And in Heb 2:10 "For it became him, for whom are all things, and by whom are all things, in bringing many sons unto glory, to make the captain of their salvation perfect through sufferings." Christ, our true example, had to be confronted by the devil, as the **Spirit** drove him into the wilderness to be tested. After forty days without food, the devil came to tempt him at his most vulnerable, weak moment. He was tempted on all three human levels: body, soul and spirit. The lust of the eye (body); the lust of the flesh (soul); and the pride of life (spirit) I John 2:16.

The devil tempted Jesus through his body appetites to lust for outer sufficiency to satisfy himself as if he were an outer, needy person: "Command this stone that it be made bread." Jesus answered out of inner fullness, not as if he were just an outer soul and body with outer needs. His meat and inner supply was the truth of what God says. Secondly, the devil tempted Jesus on his soul, intellectual and performing level. Satan made it sound only logical, as he played on his fleshly desire to perform: "**If** you are the son of God, then jump off this cliff and an angel will save you." This is always the devil's way of reasoning: "If what you say is true, then you must prove it by performing." Jesus simply answered by saying, "Thou shall not tempt the Lord thy God." In other words, he was who He said he was, and He didn't have to prove it by performance.

Then lastly, the devil tempted him on his spirit level, with the lust for power and dominion. Satan actually offered him the kingdoms of this world. How could he claim all the world powers as his own? It is clear that God has given him rule over all the world systems, for I John 5:19 says, "the whole world lieth in the lap of the wicked one."

As the final exposure of Satan came, Jesus would not see himself separate from God. Satan gave himself away by saying "worship and serve me." In other words, "Jesus, your flesh (or your created form) is lord and master, serve it and you will serve and worship me." Now Jesus saw what the tempter was really after. He wanted the human Jesus to become the son of Satan, instead of the son of God. As the son of Satan he would operate as Satan, and become a self-for-self. His spirit center would then become self-centered, saving himself and not dying on the Cross. With Satan's true purpose exposed, Jesus could boldly say, "Get behind me Satan, for I shall worship the Lord thy God, and him only shall I serve."

God used his necessary agent, Satan, to confront His son, and finally fix him in the self-knowledge of sonship. Then and only then could the Spirit anoint his humanity with the power to carry out his ministry for the next three years. Luke 4:13, says, "The devil departed from him for a season," making it clear that Jesus was hounded by Satan probably the rest of his life. Hebrews 2:18 says, "It behooved him to be made like unto his brethren, that he might be a merciful and faithful high priest in things pertaining to God, to make reconciliation for the sins of the people. For in that he himself hath suffered being tempted, he is able to keep them that are tempted."

Then the final temptation came as he was preparing for his death. Just think: he had prophesied of his upcoming death and resurrection all through his ministry, yet at the final hour he was pulled into great fear, so much so that he sweat great drops of blood. Matthew and Luke tell us that his soul was exceedingly sorrowful unto death. He cried out to his father to save him, "If thou will take this cup from me, nevertheless not as I will, but as thou will."

Notice that in a temptation we are pulled to see separation. Just earlier he had said to Philip, "If you see me, you see the Father" (John 14:9). Now he was pulled to believe he had two wills. I believe he was really saying, "not what I am tempted to want on a soul level, but rather, what I really want is what my Father wants for me on a spirit level where we are joined as one." Obviously, this went against all of his soul level feelings, as he discerned the difference between his soul pulls and the true reality of spirit.

Notice also that his only defense against Satan's attacks was to say his word of faith. We simply speak the truth and the lie will lose its false strength. Otherwise, if we fight, we believe in it as a separate reality and give it false powers. When we come into a dark room, we don't fight the darkness, we accept it. For what we fight, we empower. The answer is to simply turn on the light and the darkness, which is only the absence of light, is swallowed up.

The Lord showed this to me some years ago at a meeting where there was lots of confusion. Since I was the next speaker, I asked for the Lord's wisdom. The answer came to me clearly: "**Do not try to untangle the lie; speak the truth and the lie will untangle itself.** But if you try to clarify the confusion, you will get entangled yourself." Jesus did not fight his temptation, He simply recognized His oneness with His Father's will.

Did Jesus move from that garden, therefore, to try to fulfill his Father's will? No, he simply stood on his weak word of faith and waited for the strength to swallow up his weakness, as the light swallows up its necessary opposite, darkness. The negative puts passion and strength behind the positive thrust forward. I always say it's like a sling shot; the negative pull back gives strength to the positive. Hebrews 9:14 says, "Through the eternal **Spirit** he offered himself without spot to God." So, the Holy Spirit rose up in Christ with victorious strength, and he went to the Cross as a king. "Not by power, or by strength, but by my Spirit saith the Lord" (Zechariah 4:6).

It was totally necessary for Jesus to be tempted by Satan in the wilderness, as well as in the garden. These temptations showed Jesus that as a human he had no power to operate apart from the Father within. That is why he could say twice in one chapter, "Of myself I can do nothing" (John 5:19&30).

13.
Daily Weaknesses

"Therefore I take pleasure in infirmities, in reproaches, in necessities, in persecutions, in distresses for Christ's sake: for when I am weak then am I strong."
(II Corinthians 12:10)

Darkness is the absence of light and the right ground of our being, for it greatly hungers after its opposite--light, just as weakness is the opposite, but necessary, mate to strength. Without it we wouldn't know faith. Since we are continually tempted in daily life, surely we are also continually weak. Weakness in daily life is spoken of in II Corinthians 12 as Paul's glory. As a matter of fact, it was Satan in Paul's flesh that God used as his "thorn in the flesh."

The Lord had no intention of delivering Paul from this temptation, for Satan was God's helper to cause Paul to know weakness in his flesh. Paul had great revelation, and along with great revelation comes great weaknesses. For "to whom much is given, much is required"(Luke 12:48). Weakness is God's tool to keep us **safe.** II Corinthians 1:9 says, "we have the sentence of death in ourselves, that we should not trust in ourselves, but in God." This sentence of death is designed to make us see that we are not "sufficient of ourselves to think anything as of ourselves; but our sufficiency is of **God**" (II Corinthians 3:5). Any of us could be tempted to have pride as if we were something of ourselves. If God did not bless us with weaknesses as His way of keeping us safe, we would all fall into the prideful trap of taking the credit. But the question remains, how do we handle our weaknesses?

Paul did not stop short, as so many Christians do, by trying to fight Satan, God's appointed messenger. No! Instead, he gloried in his weaknesses as **God's calling card to faith.** He saw that God's grace was made perfect in weakness (II Cor. 12:10). He caught the glory in his weaknesses, in infirmities, in reproaches, in necessities, in persecutions, in distresses, for: "when I am weak, then am I strong." The Interlinear Greek-English New Testament actually says this: "For I am weak, then powerful I am." **Our weakness is really God's power in reverse**. The only way that God's power can be realized or expressed in this dimension is through weakness. For nothing can be known, except by its opposite. That is the law of being. Strength then, swallows up its necessary opposite, weakness, and expresses itself as the mighty power of God.

Weakness is a point of contact for the positive (God) to come through, for **pain heralds his coming**. Most people want to get out of their pain and fears, when God needs these very negative channels to manifest his positive through. **Self-acceptance is the answer.** Embrace your negative instead of trying to rid yourself of it, and you will find your release.

The acid test of faith is given in II Corinthians 13:4-5. Paul admonishes us to examine ourselves and see if we be in the faith. Then he gives us Christ as an example: "For though he was crucified through weakness, yet He lived by the power of God. For we also are **weak in him,** but we shall live with him by the power of God." Paul is clearly saying here that weakness is **"in Him"** and the very proof of faith in the Christian, for without it we would never need to believe.

I love the great scriptures in I Corinthians 1:18-29; they tell us that the preaching of the Cross is foolishness to the wise men of this world. Yet the foolishness and weakness of God is His crucified Son, and ironically, the resurrected Son is the very power of God unto them that believe. Little did we fools know, "the foolishness of God is wiser than men, and the weakness of God is stronger than men." For the weakness of God is the crucified Son, which brings about the greatest power in the universe, the resurrected and ascended Son in us. Even today, our Lord dies in weakness through his body members, that he might rise again and gain intercession for his people yet bound.

14.
Temptation

"Blessed is the man that endureth temptation: for when he is tried, he shall receive the crown of life, which the Lord hath promised to them that love him."
(James 1:12)

We human beings are tripartite: spirit, soul, and body (I Thes 5:23). God unites himself with our spirit (created in his image), for he is Spirit (John 4:24). The two become a single unity which is my "I am" (I Cor. 6:17). The soul and body are the means of expressing the "I am," it's clothing. Our spirit ("I am") is the seat of desire (heart), knowledge (mind), and choice (will). Love is expressed from the **heart.** It is either Satan's self-for-self love, or Christ's selfless love. We **know** in our spirits either the wisdom from this world (Satan's mind), or the wisdom of God (the mind of Christ). Our **will** chooses our destiny under the direction of our heart and mind.

Our spirit is the control center for the rest of our being. We either have the Holy Spirit united to our spirits, desiring his desires (Proverbs 11:23), knowing his own wisdom (I Cor. 2:16) and choosing his actions (Phil. 2:13), or we contain the spirit of this world (Satan) Eph. 2:2-3, expressing the opposite nature.

Our soul is our individual unique personalities with thinking (reason and logic) and feeling (emotional likes or dislikes) capacities. In the garden of Eden "man became a living soul." He was a created being with life, yet this life was not created to operate of itself. That is why Paul's examples of the human being are characterized as simple vessels (Romans 9:22,23).

This soul life of ours is actively thinking ideas, feeling emotional moods, or planning reasonable strategies. Our souls are somewhat like a two way mirror which reflect from the inside of us, out, or receive from the outside of us, in. And our bodies house our soul and spirit and create a medium for outer expression.

Romans 12:2 says "be not conformed to this world, but be ye transformed by the renewing of your minds, that you may prove what is the good, and acceptable, and perfect will of God." The world pours onto us from the outside. We are not to be conformed to it (soul feelings), but we are to renew our minds to what God says (spirit knowing) about the situation. So our soul is not our thermometer for the truth, our spirit knowing is our guide to truth. This is a source of so much confusion in Christians. We often confuse our soul feelings for Spirit reality.

Sometime ago, someone called and asked to stay with me for a month. I didn't feel like I was up to it (**not condemned**). So I took the **liberty** to try to get out of it. As time went on, I could see that it was meant to be, so I had to renew my mind to the real truth of the situation. I said to the Lord, "I am not **feeling** up to doing this and I'm not sure that I even **like** the person coming (soul feelings), but You are love and You live in me, so I am love to him (spirit), and I expect to experience it as soon as I see him." God's unconditional love did come, and the man was greatly blessed.

Our souls' reactions come from our human responses to outer stimuli and are neutral in themselves. Responding negatively or positively does not constitute a **spirit** choice, for it is in our spirits that we choose sin or righteousness. Here is where we Christians are so confused. Most of us think that our response or reactions to Satan's pulls are evil and sinful in themselves. But if we, as persons, had no place to survey possibilities, we wouldn't be free people, we would be robots.

We must be free in our fleshly reactions, otherwise we would continually think of ourselves as sinners. This is why I hear so many Christians say that they are "saved sinners." That is not true! God does not call his precious blood-bought children sinners, He calls us his saints.

We are meant to be fully human and have honest reactions, otherwise we would always be suppressing our right humanity. We Christians become frustrated, trying to keep our reactions under control, and as a result we usually end up being phony. Many times Christians go into deep depressions just because they suppress normal human responses. I have heard psychologists say, for example, that depression is suppressed, inverted anger.

Personally, I was in such a sin mind set that I confessed sin continually, trying to get rid of my suppressed human reactions (which are not sin)! Finally, after finding myself confessing things that were not even true, just to get rid of my guilty feelings, I gave up. This led me to make a pact with God. I said to the Lord, "I am just going to be me, and I am not going to call anything sin (excluding the obvious) unless you tell me." I knew that God was big enough to take a sledge hammer and hit me over the head if he wanted me to know. Otherwise, I was going to live freely in the green light, not cautiously in the yellow, or stopped by the red.

Jesus certainly never suppressed his humanity, for He was totally true to himself. When he was angry at the Pharisees (Matthew 23) he knew that his was right anger. But when he was crying out to God in the garden, "take this cup from me," he knew that he was being tempted. The point here is to just be yourself and trust God for the discernment.

Temptation is not sin! And we **must** know the difference. James 1:14 says, "Every man is tempted when he is drawn away of his own lust and enticed." Lust isn't evil in itself, for it is God-given desire. But Satan tries to entice us through it to believe that we really want what we should not have. This period of enticement is not sin, but temptation. When Satan tempted Jesus in the wilderness by offering him all the kingdoms of the world, there had to be a part of Jesus that wanted these kingdoms or it would not have been a temptation. Yet Jesus didn't call these satanic pulls "sin."

The next verse goes on to say, "When lust hath **conceived**, it bringeth forth sin"(James 1:15). The thing that most Christians don't understand is that sinning (conception by the will) is really hard to do. It's somewhat like raping your own nature; you have to go against your own heart and turn your back on God's keeping power. Sinning is possible, but not probable. But if temptation does become sin, the Christian temporarily joins with Satan in an adulterous affair which brings forth sin. But we can praise God for his provision, the shed blood of his Son, and faith in that fact will cleanse us totally.

Temptation is our daily diet, while sin is very rare. Temptation is an enticement to want to do evil, while sin is a spirit choice of **"I will."** We resist evil by **not** fighting it, but by replacing the lie with the truth of who we really are. Christ in us is pure desire, not misused lust or perverted desire. This surrendering to God, by faith, as our keeper makes Satan flee from us (James 4:7).

Sometimes temptation makes me feel stormy and dark on the inside. My soul-feelings remind me of a whirling, dark tornado. Jesus also felt that way, "My soul is exceedingly sorrowful unto death." If I fight these reactions, then I am caught in the darkness without clarity. But if I dare accept my stormy feelings as meant by God, and **go with them,** then I will get the clarity to see that there is really a perfectly calm place of peace inside of me, which is in the eye of the tornado. That is a good picture of the difference between my stormy **soul** reactions and the real **spirit** me that is peaceful. No matter how stormy it gets, the storm cannot touch the perfect peace of the eye, which is where I really live. If I get confused, thinking that my soul storms are me, then I am caught. But if I dare leap into the truth of who I am, I will rest in the midst of my tornado.

If we hate ourselves for our soul reactions, we are like a soldier going out to battle, but fighting the wrong thing. Foolishly hating our soul reactions is like fighting the battlefield. No soldier would do that. Our souls are the battlefields of Satan's attacks, and not the enemy. Yet we Christians spend our time hating ourselves (our souls) for feeling or thinking evil thoughts, instead of recognizing that the real evil is not coming from us, but from Satan. It helps me to remember that Satan is **on** us but not **in** us. Our final liberation comes when we can put these satanic temptations in their proper perspective and back into God as his necessary negative training ground for us, and our opportunity for faith.

15.
"Simple Toward Evil"

"I would have you wise unto that which is good, but simple toward evil."
(Romans 16:19)

I want to quote two scriptures that are very powerful to me: the first one Paul uses at the end of his epistle to the Romans, and the second is in the old Testament; "Be wise unto that which is good and **simple concerning evil**" (16:19) and, "Thou shall **not see evil any more**" (Zeph. 3:15).

When I quote these scriptures, people often think that my view of evil is somewhat like Scarlet O'Hara's, "I'll think about it tomorrow," outlook. They think I'm denying the very existence of evil. But when Jesus told his disciples to "be wise as serpents and harmless as doves," he didn't mean for them to have a "New Age" understanding of evil, that is, not seeing it anymore by **denying** its existence.

"Wise as a serpent" means that we have a full understanding of the very nature of evil without giving it false credit by believing **in** it, as if it were a separate power independent from God. Faith in the supreme sovereignty of God means that we don't deny evil's existence, but we do deny its power or authority as it appears separated from God. If evil can act separately from God, then it has an existence apart from God's purposes. God forbid! For if this were true, we all would be without hope.

It means that even though we see evil as a reality in our outer world, we fit evil, as well as good, back into the one person in the universe, God, the All in All. Thus, evil is rightly seen as the **necessary servant of God** who means and "works all things after the counsel of His own will" (Eph. 1:11).

Faith people are often called **"see-throughers, instead of see-at-ers."** As a see-througher (which is the same thing as having a "single eye" of faith) we can then truly catch the glory and adventure of faith in the **present** tense, by not seeing the false power of evil anymore.

The secret of seeing "God only" joins our divided consciousness and fills our whole body full of light: "If thy eye be single thy whole body is full of light" (Matt. 5:22). How does this work? Is it natural for us to see God only? No! We start out by seeing evil or double, because through the Fall we have eaten from the divided fruit of good and evil. Our old master, Satan, imparted to us a divided consciousness that vainly wrestles between warring opposites, a consciousness which is the fruit of the knowledge of good and evil.

But isn't it also true that the Bible tells us that God was the one who subjected us to this satanic rule? Yes, for it says, "The creation was subjected to frustration, not by its own choice, but by the will of the one who subjected it, in hope that the creation itself will be liberated from its bondage to decay and brought into the glorious freedom of the children of God" (Rom. 8:20).

In fact, God handed us, innocent babes, right into the hands of subtle Satan. Why would God do that? God knows that the essential nature of personhood is freedom of choice. Therefore a person **must** be faced with opposite alternatives, which was what the spirit of error had to offer, and choose between the alternatives. If we do not exercise this essential part of ourselves, we are not mature persons. We, as parents, all want our children to mature into adulthood. So then, a son of God, in order to inherit his inheritance, **must** be confronted by opposites.

Nothing can be known as a conscious reality except by it's opposite. Hot is meaningless to us without its comparative opposite, cold. Soft cannot be experienced without its opposite counterpart hard, and so on. In photography, the negative background brings out the positive foreground. If I were to photograph a polar bear in a snow storm, the bear would be hard, and maybe even impossible, to see. Yet, if the polar bear were contrasted with a dark background, he would be plainly seen.

The Bible says that, "Mortality is swallowed up, of immortality" (II Cor. 5:4). "Death is swallowed up, in life" (I Cor. 15:54); "Light is swallowed up in darkness" (II Cor. 4:6); and the "Invisible things are understood by the things that are seen" (Rom. 1:20). All of life is known by opposites. Everything in the universe functions by pairs of opposites, the one gaining definition and knowledge by its necessary opposite. Then the one opposite utilizes the other to manifest itself. This is the law of manifestation.

Adam and Eve had no more than an infantile consciousness of themselves and couldn't have really known themselves, just like a little child doesn't really know himself and has not developed into the fullness of his potential. So, in a sense, we had to know separation as our reality, as well as fully experience its consequences, in order to inwardly seek, find, and then fully know our union with God.

In the same sense, the angels in heaven cannot know the full meaning of grace because they cannot contrast it with sin. We know the grace and love of God because we first know what it means to be a sinner. **Sin gives definition to grace.**

Our Father knows that we must know the lies of a satanic self-sufficiency to the depths of our being, as well as the lie of Satan's false promises of total fulfillment apart from God. He also knew, in His wisdom, that the first man had to experience vanity as a false reality, develop it as a false independent identity, and suffer the full consequences of unbelief. Then and only then would he be conditioned to receive the opposite kingdom, of God, and know his true identity as Christ with full experiential knowledge, which is based on the life of another living in us, as us.

When we have plunged to these great satanic depths, we can, by faith in the Cross of Christ, leap from our divided consciousness of good and evil, to the heights of seeing God only. This is the fruit of the tree of Life, and such seeing fills our whole selves with illuminating light. As Matthew 6:23 says, "if your eye be single your whole body is full of light, but if your eye be evil your whole body is full of darkness, and how great is that darkness." Note that the opposite of single is double, therefore the word "evil" in this verse really must mean double. Double means seeing evil as separated from God and his purposes, which causes us to experience anguish instead of peace.

I personally learned the secret of God only through the death of my mother. The day I told her that she had cancer she said right back to me, "Sylvia, we will not give the devil one bit of glory over this. This cancer is from God--we are going to praise Him for this cancer!" In fact, one of her favorite verses was "In everything give thanks; for this is the will of God in Christ Jesus concerning you" (I Thess. 5:18).

She then explained to me why her cancer couldn't really kill her: "How can this kill me, I am already dead! The life you see here is not me, it's Christ, because He is living *as* me. So don't cry for me; this is not happening to me, it is happening to Christ!" Because she refused to see evil and lived in praise instead of self-pity, her faith transcended her pain. Her body died in weakness, but her spirit soared in victory.

16.
Seeing Through Evil to God Only!

"The Lord hath taken away thy judgments, he hath cast out thine enemy: the king of Israel, even the Lord, is in the midst of thee; thou shalt not see evil any more."
(Zephaniah 3:15)

Most of our problems come from our short-sightedness in not seeing through our negative circumstances or "evil" to God's purposes. Jesus makes a powerful statement in Matthew 11:27 by saying, "All things are delivered unto me **by my Father**." Why didn't he say that the cross was coming to him from his enemy, the devil? Wasn't it the devil's cross? Yes, it was. Yet Jesus embraced it as his "Father's cup!" Jesus looked through Satan to the Father's cup! Jesus even greeted Judas by calling him friend when Judas came with the soldiers to the garden of Gethsemane. Christ's faith transformed his enemy into his friend. Then when Peter reacted by fighting the enemy, Jesus answered by saying, "The cup which **my Father** hath **given me**, shall I not drink it?" Jesus had said earlier to Pilate, "My kingdom is not of this world: if my kingdom were of this world, then would my servants fight, that I should not be delivered to the Jews: but now is my kingdom not from hence" (John 18:36). Jesus' consciousness had changed from two wills in the garden (not my will, but thy will) to seeing God only. **He called his enemy his friend, and the devil's cross his Father's cup!**

When he faced Pilate for the second time, Pilate was enraged at his non-response. Pilate said to him, "Don't you know I have power to crucify you?" Jesus answered by saying, "You have **no** power at all against me, except it were given thee from **above**" (John 19:11). Jesus was actually saying that Pilate had no independent power to do **anything** against him except what the Father gave him to do. Earthly power is ordained from above. Jesus was saying there is only one power in the universe, and that power is his Father.

Nothing that happens is outside of God's purposes. Does that mean that God causes the evil? No. God means evil because he means man's freedom, and evil is the natural outworking of misused freedom. He knew that freedom was going to be misused. He also means the negative consequences of that misuse. In God's wisdom He then conveniently uses these negative consequences to instill self-knowledge. With this self-knowledge, we can hopefully see what causes us death and what we really don't want. A small child learns that if he touches a hot stove, it will burn him. He knows this because he has touched it previously and gotten burned.

Romans 13:1 says, "Let every soul be subject unto the higher powers. For there is **no power but God**; the powers that be are ordained of God." So Jesus, our perfect pattern, embraced his Cross instead of wasting time waging futile war against the devil. He simply saw through to His Father's cup. Isn't this what Zephaniah 3:15 means when it says, "The Lord hath taken away thy judgments, he hath cast out thine enemy: the king of Israel, even the Lord, is in the midst of thee: **thou shalt not see evil any more?**" This means that the Lord has taken away my false judgments of separation, because through the Cross, Satan (Mr. Independent-self) is cast out. Now I have a new consciousness, which is the mind of Christ, and my judgments are not separated by seeing two powers. Now I see one power in the universe, and I will not see evil separate from God anymore.

The early Christians saw it. At Peter's first sermon he states, "Him, being delivered by the determinate counsel and foreknowledge of God, ye have taken, and by wicked hands have crucified and slain" (Acts 2:23). Seeing God only does not take the responsibility of sin from off the sinner. Later in Acts 4:10, Peter, in his own defense at the trial set by the Sanhedrin, explains that **they** were responsible for crucifying Jesus. After the trial, Peter was beaten and thrown into prison. The next day he addressed the believers: "For of a truth against thy anointed, both Herod, and Pontius Pilate, with the Gentiles, and people of Israel, were gathered together, for to do whatsoever thy hand and thy council determined before to be done" (27-28). Now why did he present it differently? To the unsaved he said that **they** had crucified Jesus. But to the saved, Peter received it all from the hand of God, and gave no credit to the devil at all.

The Bible says that there is the "mystery of iniquity." God has hidden the fact that Satan is the real perpetrator of evil and is God's convenient agent. God has hidden this from the sinner because he would use this truth to justify himself. All mankind has to be guilty before God, for God uses guilt to bring mankind to repentance. If we could justify ourselves and blame our sin on God, we would, and this would keep us from facing our sins in true repentance towards God.

If the darkest most evil day in history, which was the day Jesus was put on the cross, was determined by God the Father, and seen by the Son as the Father's cup, how can we call minor evils anything less? Satan was really defeated there at the cross. Jesus said in John 12:31, "Now is the judgment of this world: now shall the prince of this world be cast out." Why do we give so much lip service to a defeated foe? Jesus didn't! The strongest thing we can do is to live in the praise of seeing God only and ignore the devil and his bluffs. This is what makes him flee! God exposes Satan by bringing him to the **foreground** in Romans 7. The purpose of this exposure is to defeat his rule in us, by putting his false authority under the finished work of Christ. Now, God conveniently uses him and he is hardly noticeable in the **background.**

Job, the oldest book in the Bible, testifies of Satan's purposes in mankind's sanctification. God drew Satan's attention to Job, God's perfect man, and then let Satan have at him. Yet Job never saw the evil coming to him as being from Satan: "Shall we receive good at the hand of God, and shall we not receive evil?" In all this Job did not sin with his lips. His single eye saw through to the One he was believing in, by faith. The latter part of Job's life was better than the beginning, because his immature consciousness was cleansed from the evil of self-sufficiency. He learned that he was the nothing, and God was the all. All this came by the single, inner eye of revelation. "I have heard of thee by the hearing of the ear: but now mine eye seeth thee" (Job 42:5).

The Other Side of Suffering

August, 1994

In the last month I have learned that my son has AIDS. I have asked **WHY HIM?** But the fact is that it is, and this has happened.

What am I going to do with this critical news? I have run the gamut of emotions...Anger...Fear...Guilt...and they have worn me out... Please God, let me transform my reactions from death to life...to love.

I am willing to be made willing to enter into this unknown living that has come upon me...I may not always feel comfortable...Hurts and thoughts pull me around...Separation from God seems so close. I cry, "This is all out of order.....my son shouldn't die before me," Yet I always sense the closeness of God....even in the very depths of hopelessness. How our beliefs can liberate us...or limit us.

Then if my son's physical healing is not in God's plan...I say this word of faith....that I thank God for his life, and savor each and every precious day with him.....I trust God with both life and death.....my son's life is poured out wine for others. Is it the caterpillar's end, or the butterfly's beginning?

November 1995

I have experienced going bankrupt...I've been moved by great music and art. I've been humiliated ....embarrassed, blessed....and cursed at various times in my life! But I have never experienced the 'heart rendering' sorrow.....the indescribable suffering of losing my son...his life snuffed out like a candle before its time....so loving...so handsome...so full of dreams, and more importantly, so loving and thoughtful of others. The many memories I have of him fill my eyes so with tears; an aching heart that almost refuses to be consoled. This is deep like a hole in my very being....it's permanent and can't be healed....I want to shut myself away choosing misery.....Bitterness and cynicism seems to crouched at my door....My soul.....Is this the answer I sometimes cry out? Why was I made?....Take this 'cup' from me?

This suffering is like trying to cross a river that one must go through torrents and emotional currents to get to the other side....Could there be another side of suffering? I know that this is something which all of us know or will....It's universal....So for me the only place to turn is to God...I remember the scripture where Jesus said, blessed are they that mourn, for they shall be comforted. What could that mean? And then I discover that comfort, by definition, in Latin, means to 'strengthen,' I know that on the other side of suffering a strength has been brought about in me.

I am comforted by knowing...By saying just to myself...By saying aloud...That from suffering comes results. This I've seen...A new tenderness..Healing of hurts and misunderstanding...New loving relationships....But, above all...The eyes to see God in the middle of it all, knowing that He is a loving God. That in my weakness,' He is strength. Our God doesn't witness to the world by taking us out of pain and suffering but, by demonstrating himself in the midst of it all. The life and death of Jesus was for other. I say that the life and death of my son is for others. The Lord has shown me that out of death...Always comes life! I remember the story of the seed that falls in the earth dead.....Yet, in the spring behold a new growth has begun and life comes forth.

Death does not have the final word...So I take heart in my Brokenness...Knowing that God mends...I am willing to discover the value of my son's death...Like the candle...Ready to be re-lit at any moment to help others see their way through their period of darkness...Thus, we become part of the 'Light' that lights the way to eternal life. **God Only!**

These letters were written by my dear friend, Vangie Leidgen in memory of her son Kurt.

17. Calling Into Being That Which Does Not Exist

"I have made thee a father of many nations, before him whom he believed, even God, who quickeneth the dead, and calleth those things which be not as though they were."
(Romans 4:17)

Harriet Wearren is one of the strongest faith people that I know. I want to share her amazing and courageous story of faith. It is pure glory and "Holy Ground." There is no way that I could begin to write it, so I asked Harriet to write this chapter in the book.

~~~~~~~~~

I grew up in a loving family with a younger sister, a strong spiritual mother, and a father who was a good man: an intelligent, interesting person, but an alcoholic. I loved my family, but I was very angry and disappointed with my father.

We went every Sunday to the Presbyterian Church, and I prayed that God would change my dad so that our lives would be normal--like everyone else's. I suppose I always had great and high expectations for my family members and for myself, and was always looking for something to change so I could be totally happy! Right after high school I met a handsome, fun loving young man and fell in love. We dated for two years and married after my sophomore year of college. In my mind I thought, "Cinderella has met the handsome prince, and they will live happily ever after." I stayed in school to get my degree, but my main ambition was to be a good wife and become a mother.

Failure was almost immediate. Who could live up to my expectations? I couldn't and neither could Wade. What a heavy burden to put on another person! I was extremely frustrated. There was a void in my life that only God could fill, but at that time, I thought if I tried harder, and Wade would try harder, everything would be fine.

Things did not get any easier. We graduated from college and our daughter Beth was born in September. We loved being parents, but it added to my frustration, because now, I not only was demanding time for myself with Wade, but also with the baby. I wanted us to have the "perfect family life." Four years after Beth, our son Scott was born, and then a few years later we had Andrew. It became increasingly difficult to do all the things that needed to be done to keep the family running smoothly. Wade had a job that kept him out of town five days a week and he would come home on the weekends. I would look forward all week to his homecoming, but would meet him at the door with all my frustrations, and rail at him! He was a great father and did lots with the kids, but it was never quite enough for me.

Wade, of course, was not feeling any more fulfilled than I was. He began to withdraw in little ways, and then he began to search for his fulfillment everywhere except at our house. It was driving me crazy, but we couldn't talk about it because Wade could never discuss personal problems and try to work them out. We were ready to divorce!

One night when I could not sleep because I was so desperate, I knew I was one step away from Our Lady of Peace (the mental hospital in Louisville). I opened my bible and put my finger on the page to see if God could or would show me anything. Really, I hardly believed it would work, but when I looked to see where my finger was, it was Matthew 11:27, "All things come to me from my Father's hand." Somehow I knew this was directly to me from God and I believed it.

I was attending a small bible study at that time, trying to fit all the pieces of my life together, and one day I read, "In everything give thanks, for this is the will of God in Christ Jesus concerning you" (I Thess. 5:18). I realized that everything that happened in my life came from God, the good and the bad. The Bible says, "God is love" (I John 4:16), so everything that comes in life, comes from His loving hand. Although I may not always see it, there is a reason and constructive purpose in everything.

Our situation did not change as I began to learn these things, but the way I looked at the situation did change. It was a miracle! As bad as things were between Wade and me, I felt God was pressing me to say that **everything** in my life came from Him and that I was to be **thankful** for everything. I felt that God was pressing me to believe that Wade would find his fulfillment in God and that our marriage was whole and complete, although this really seemed to be far from the truth. But I had to believe that God would "find" Wade, even though he was not knowingly looking for God. God is a big God, so much bigger than our finite minds can imagine. Is anything too big or too hard for Him?

Romans 4:17 became imprinted on my heart as the Holy Spirit revealed His truth to me. "We call the things that are not, as though they are." This is the story of Abraham, who simply believed God, and is called the "father of our faith" because of it. God told Abraham when he was an old man that he would be the father of many nations, that his descendants would be numbered as many as the stars in the heavens and as the sands of the sea. Sarah, his wife, was much too old to conceive, so it was laughable to think this could really happen. But in due time, Isaac was born, because

Abraham had believed and trusted God. **God impressed upon my heart to do the same with my situation.**

While all of this was taking place, our three children were growing up. Our middle child, Scott, was in first grade when we found that our bright precious child could not learn to read. We found out that he had a severe learning problem called dyslexia, and I became very protective of him. He was so happy on week-ends, but all hell would break loose on Monday morning when he had to go back to school. I nearly went crazy! One time, I thought I'd like to gather all of us in the house and put dynamite to it and just blow us all up. I was at the end of my rope. I had a degree in elementary education and couldn't even help my own child!

Finally, when Scott was in the second grade, I found The dePaul School, a school for children with dyslexia, and went to look at it. It was so structured and disciplined that it looked awful to me. I argued with God all the way home. I said that I loved Scott too much to subject him to that harsh school, it would be the end of him. Since I had searched everywhere and this was the **only** place I was able to find, I knew that God was asking if I loved him enough to give him this chance. I was learning about the love of God. It is not a protective love that keeps you totally tucked away, in a box, but it is a love that pushes you out into the unknown. Well, shock of all shocks, the place that I thought would be the end of Scott, was the very place he blossomed.

About this time, a missionary came to visit the lady who taught our bible study and a group of us went to hear him speak. He told us there is only One person in the universe. In the beginning that was such a puzzle to me, but slowly I came to realize what he meant. Everything in this world is a form of God. He is love poured out for His created universe. He spoke of Galatians 2:20 which says, "I am crucified with Christ, nevertheless I live, but it is no longer I who live, but Christ who lives in me." What consolation this was to me when I finally understood it.

The good news to me was--"It is not me living here, but Christ living my life." If I am washing the dishes, driving the carpool, etc. it is Christ who is living in me, who is doing all the things I do.

While I was learning this, I felt schizophrenic half the time. The things I did that looked good were easy to call God, but with my fiery temper, the things I did that didn't look so nice kept me very confused. Finally one day, when I was giving my kids a bath, Beth did something that shoved me over the edge. I jerked her out of the tub by her hair and immediately felt such awful remorse. I thought it despicable that I would dare to say that Christ was in me, living my life, and act in such an awful way. As I walked into the hall I said to myself, "What I am believing is either true all the time or none of the time." I had to say, "I'm daring to believe that you are here living my life no matter how I look." It was a turning point for me to keep my eyes on God and not on how I appeared.

I came to realize that the seed of Christ is in every man. We are born with it, but it has to come to birth in us. Because it had been birthed in me, I could look at all the loved ones who needed to know this for themselves. I began with the verse in I Cor. 7:14, "For the unbelieving husband is **sanctified** by the wife, and the unbelieving wife is sanctified by the husband." Then from there to Jude 24, "Now unto him that is able to keep you from falling, and to present you faultless before the presence of his glory with exceeding joy."

I did the same for Wade that I had done for myself. I stopped looking at his appearance and just kept affirming what God had already done in him. Most of the time it looked hopeless, and when I would say this to God, He would let me know that He was tending to His business and that I should tend to mine. My part was to simply believe by faith, and His part was to change Wade from the **inside out**.

After years of battle, we came to know that everything that happens in our lives, happens for a reason. All of Wade's past was perfect for him to come to know that his life is not his own. He finally saw that he was a "O" (zero), but that God was the "all" inside of him. What a relief that was for Wade, who thought he had to make himself be better and turn himself around—when all he had to do was trust that God was working it all out. He was waiting for Wade to come to the end of his trying. God has given Wade such insight, wisdom, and empathy for people who are caught in the most severe problems and He has a way of bringing those people into Wade's life.

Everything that happened in my life before July 27, 1982 was the perfect preparation of my spirit for what happened that day.

I woke up early, as usual, and got Wade and Scott, now 17 years old, off to work. Scott came back home about an hour later looking for a radio for the truck he was trading in that day on a "new" used car. He was so excited. Shortly after he left, Linda Bunting, my good friend and next door neighbor, came bursting in to tell me there had been a terrible accident and Scott was being taken to the hospital. I went upstairs and put some clothes on, because I was still in my robe. As I went into my room, I thought to myself, "I know I'm a strong person of faith, but will my faith be big enough for this?" I was gripped by fear! Into my mind came the verse in II Timothy 2:13, "Even if we believe not, He abideth faithful, for He will not deny Himself." What a relief. It wasn't even my faith, it was His faith. It wasn't up to me. I knew God would get us through whatever lay ahead, and He would do it His way.

Linda stopped to pick up Sylvia Pearce, our other friend and neighbor, on the way to the hospital. I was shocked that I was so calm. I thought about a friend of ours who had a severe heart condition which required open heart surgery. It looked as though he would not survive, but God gave me a verse for him, Romans 4:18, "Against hope, they believed in hope," and I knew in my heart he was going to make it, and he did. On the way to the hospital to see about Scott, I presented the same verse for him, but I knew it didn't fit. The verse that came to me was, "It **pleased** God to bruise His Son" (Isa. 53:10). I only asked one thing of God--not to leave Scott a vegetable. I felt he had had struggle enough all those years with dyslexia and he would hate not being able to take care of himself. So I told God that I was willing to give him up, but I expected--no, I **demanded** to see life come from his death. Then my mind turned to organ donation and all the things I had thought through the years about how that would be the thing to do, if he wasn't going to make it.

When we got to the hospital, Scott was still alive, but barely. I told them immediately that I did not want him kept alive on life support, but they told me he was holding his own. Linda's husband, John Bunting, is a surgeon. He had met us there and was with Scott. How sweet of God to have someone who loved him as much as we did, be there with him. I called our other two children, Beth and Andrew, to tell them that Scott was still alive. Beth had gotten on the phone and called some of our Christian friends around the country to let them know what had happened. I call it rallying the faithful, because what we needed right that moment was prayer--we had it from everywhere!

We had not been in the emergency room long when John came to tell me Scott had taken a turn for the worse. His head injuries were severe. I told the doctor that I would like to donate any organs, but that needed consent from both parents. When we asked Wade, who had never thought of it before, he was so grief stricken he didn't want to do it. Shortly thereafter, he changed his mind, but it was too late for everything except Scott's corneas. That was the beginning of the life that came from Scott's death. It's a principle of God. Someone else would have sight because Scott lost his. I called the children back and told them Scott had died. I told them we could feel really sad for ourselves, but we had to feel happy for Scott because it was his birthday into heaven!

When our children are born, we think they belong to us, but the truth is, they are a gift from God. "He holds the keys to life and death" and we look at death differently than

God. Death is merely moving into the next phase of eternal life--a new beginning, not an end. We are more familiar with the physical part of us than with the spiritual, but it's the spirit that does not die.

We left the hospital and went home to make funeral preparations and to cope with a life that would never ever be the same again. It was unbelievable. Like magic--one minute Scott was here and life was normal, the next minute he was gone! And our lives were forever changed.

It began to come to me that there is a time, appointed of God, that each of us will die. God knows better than I do, what is best for each of us. I was thankful that my dad, who loved Scott very much, had died two years before. He was there in heaven waiting for Scott, as well as all the other loved ones who had died.

Our friends and relatives came to our house to offer their love and support. It meant so much to us to have them there. Some of the people who came had walked this road before us. They were especially helpful. I marveled that these people who had lost a child, were still functioning and their lives were going on. Bless their hearts for being there for us!

I was at perfect peace, and decided I must be in shock. When I said this to my sister-in-law, she looked at me so funny and said, "Is it shock or is it your faith?" I knew she was right--God's faith had risen in me!

I had been in a bible study for a couple of years with some women who had lost children. They had founded a group in Louisville called Compassionate Friends for parents who have lost a child. Through the years I had said some very hard things to them, such as, "In everything give thanks, for this is the will of God in Christ Jesus concerning you" (I Thess. 5:18). When I would leave these women I'd feel terrible and say to myself, "What if this happened to you? How would you like to hear that?" I could only believe that was exactly what I would want to hear, and I found this was true. My heart leapt to the spirit's truths.

Our wonderful friends, Barbara and Dan Stone, came to be with us. Dan did the funeral service. It was beautiful, and he said everything I would have wanted to say.

At the funeral home a friend handed me a poem she had found in the paper. It was wonderful and remains a joy to me every time I read it:

> I am standing on the seashore. A ship spreads her sails to the morning breeze and starts for the ocean. I stand watching, until she fades from the horizon, and someone at my side says, She's gone. Gone? Where? The loss of sight is in me, not in her. Just at the moment when someone says she is gone, there are others who are watching her coming. Other voices take up the glad shout,
> Here She Comes!
> And that is dying.

The reason I love it so much is that it affirms that life doesn't end with death, it is merely changed! But, we are in the physical dimension, so we are unable to see the Spirit dimension.

Little did I know, the day of the funeral, that harder days were to come. After everything settled down and people began to live their normal lives again, we were left alone to find a new kind of normal for us, because our lives would never be the same again. I was shocked to find how hard everyday tasks were: waking up every morning to be hit again with the words in my head, "Scott is dead"; going to the grocery and being overwhelmed with loss as I pass the apple cider that I always bought by the gallon because Scott loved it; even sitting at the kitchen table to have a meal was so hard, because one person was obviously missing. I knew the holidays would be hard, but I didn't know how hard everyday life would be.

Immediately following Scott's accident, which was about a mile and a half from our house, I decided I would never drive past the accident sight again. I didn't know how I could stand it. This was going to present a hardship because that was the most convenient way to and from our house. I finally decided that there is a time appointed of God that we all will die and the place and circumstance is beside the point. The point is that it is God's appointed time for the person! I knew that I need not be held in bondage to that spot in the road, so I had a friend drive me past it while I closed my eyes. Then I drove myself, averting my eyes, and finally I could drive by and even take a look. It was such a beautiful, benign looking place that it was hard to believe such a life-changing event had happened there.

We had good days and bad days, and I realized that this was normal. One particularly hard day, I was so depressed I could hardly move. I had to go to the mall and happened to get there before the stores opened. As I sat there watching people go by, I felt so sorry for myself. Everyone looked so peaceful and happy, and I resented the fact that their lives were wonderful and ours was in shambles. The doors to the store opened, and as I got up to enter the store, I caught my reflection in the plate glass window and was shocked to see that I looked just like them. I could not believe that I looked so normal. The way I felt, I should have had scars all over my face, but I didn't. I then took another look at the people all around me who looked so "normal" and wondered what kind of scars must they have that did not show. It certainly took my attention off of me!

It took awhile, but we finally ordered a stone to mark Scott's grave. I guess it was hard to face the finality of seeing his name in stone with birth and death dates. I had thought and thought about a verse to put on the stone and finally it came to me. It was perfect: II Corinthians 4:18: "The things which are seen are temporary, but the things which are not seen are eternal." Eternal--without beginning or end. The spirit of Scott Hampton Wearren was and ever will be. "He is not a past memory, but a living presence!"

~~~~~~~~~~~~~~~

P.S. From Sylvia

My husband, Scott Pearce, was counseling a very intellectual man once, and during the session Scott asked him what faith meant to him. The man thought a minute, then quoted a verse of scripture. Scott said, "That is right, but what does faith mean to you **personally**?" The man couldn't answer. Scott continued, "Well, let me tell you what faith means to me. The summer that Scott Wearren died I was in a state of depression. Then, when I heard of his death, it grieved me even more. So I pleaded with the Lord. 'Why did you take this fine young man, and leave **me** here. I'm the one that is miserable. Why wouldn't you take **me** instead?' After a hesitation, the Lord came back with this startling answer, "It was **because** of you that I took Scott Wearren, for he paid the price of his life **for you**!" I was broken and humbled beyond words. Soon after that, I shared the incident with Harriet. "Do you want to know what her response was?" "Yes," said the man. Harriet said, "Well Scott, **you** are worth it!" She was saying that **I** was worth the death of **her** son. Now that, my friend, is what faith means to me."

"Great is the mystery of suffering; yet this much we know; suffering is in the very warp and woof of the slow progress of mankind from the vanity of time to the riches of eternity. So deeply interwoven into the stuff of things, that the very Captain of our salvation, in order to be made like unto His brethren had to made perfect through suffering. Borne rebelliously, it works death, born courageously, it unifies; borne vicariously, it helps to redeem.

All men taste of it, the innocent with the guilty; but not till the Creator was crucified was there placed within reach of a groaning and groping humanity, not indeed the full explanation of suffering, but at least the key to its transmutation. We have to learn that faith transforms the messenger of Satan into the means of grace. That believers are to glory in tribulations, count trials all joy, because all things work together for good to them that love God. And God's soldiers are to see in their crosses the mystery of the birth-process, whereby death works in us, but life in others, for only the corn of wheat which falls into the ground and dies bears "much fruit."

Taken from one of Norman Grubb's books, entitled: <u>Alfred Buxton of the Congo and Abyssinia</u>, pages 76-77.

18.

The Meaning of Suffering

"For I reckon that the sufferings of this present time are not worthy to be compared with the glory which shall be revealed in us."
(Romans 8:18)

None of us like suffering, yet it is inescapable! We might ask the question, "Why isn't everyone healthy, wealthy and wise?" Or at least, shouldn't Christians live in prosperity, since we are the children of God and rightful heirs to the kingdom? I think that this is one of the biggest misconceptions in American Christianity. The Bible says very little about outer prosperity for the Christian. On the contrary, Jesus demands the opposite. He says in Matt. 16:24 "If any man will come after me, let him deny himself, and take up his cross, and follow me. For whosoever will save his life shall lose it: and whosoever will lose his life for my sake shall find it." And Luke 14:27 says, "Whosoever doth not bear his Cross, and come after me, cannot be my disciple." This simply means that unless we take up our share of suffering, we cannot even be his disciples. Strong isn't it? Yet the greatest victory chapter of the Bible, Romans 8, is filled with suffering.

All Christianity knows that if we can live and walk in Romans 8 as a present tense reality, we have reached the zenith of Christian living. Yet, what we don't know is that its golden streets are lined with suffering. Paul starts off in verse (17) by saying that we cannot know our glorious sonship unless we have suffered with him. We cannot reign in life or know His glory without suffering. For reigning and glory go hand in hand with pain and suffering; they are the opposite ends of the same thing. But take heart, for he goes on to say that the sufferings "are not worthy to be compared with glory which shall be revealed *in us*."

Suffering and groaning (verse 22) is in **all** creation, for it waits for its release from bondage to its glorious liberation. Then Paul goes on to say that even we, the firstfruits of many brethren, are being conformed into the image of the son by the things we suffer. Paul tells us that we are not delivered **from** evil, but delivered **unto** evil, like "sheep to the slaughter." But while in the midst of this suffering "we are more than conquerors." And "if he spared not his own son, how shall he not give us **all** things." "All things" doesn't just mean the positive part of life, it means both positives and **negatives**, because you cannot know glory without suffering. We are appointed to our daily Crosses, and true victorious living is resurrection in our spirits right in the midst of our outer sufferings.

The book of II Corinthians is filled with examples of Paul's suffering, "As the sufferings of Christ abound in us"(1:15); "Paul was so troubled in Asia that it pressed him out of measure above strength, inasmuch that he despaired even of life"(1:8); "We had the sentence of death in ourselves that we should not trust in ourselves, but in God"(3:5); "no rest in my soul"(2:13); "our flesh had no rest, but we were troubled on every side, without were fighting's, within were fears" (7:5). And then in chapter 4 Paul says, "troubled, distressed, perplexed, persecuted, cast down, dying of the Lord Jesus, always delivered unto death, for death works in us" (8-12). **So why should we as Christians expect a life free from suffering?**

In a review of the play "Shadowlands" (the life story of C. S. Lewis), Kristina Halvorson wrote, "How does one begin to reconcile the seeming injustice of suffering with a living God? World-renown author, scholar, and Christian apologist C.S. Lewis seemed to have an answer: **'Pain is God's megaphone to rouse a deaf world.'**

"According to his personal doctrine, pain is what awakens us from the dream that all is well with the world. Suffering is a gift from God to keep us alert and on our toes, to keep us from falling asleep in our day-to-day lives. God sends each of us pain and suffering to shake our selfishness and illusion that all is well. For only after this illusion is smashed, will people actively seek salvation in God, knowing the **'true good lies in another world,'** and this present world is no more than shadowlands."

On seeing the movie "Shadowlands" I was very impressed with some of the statements made by Anthony Hopkins, the actor portraying C.S. Lewis. "God sees us like a giant piece of granite. Every blow of life is God's chisel to sculpt out the image that he wants."

"God wants us to grow up--He wants us to get out of the nursery. Something must drive us out of the nursery and out of our own self-centeredness, and that something is **suffering**." His final statement in the movie was, "I have suffered greatly twice in my life: Once as a boy, and I chose safety, and once as a man, and I chose suffering." As a boy all he could do was choose safety for himself, and then afterwards he built a life of self protection. As a man he learned that suffering is a very viable part of life, so he embraced it, and was greatly blessed.

God cannot allow us to be satisfied in this world because our true home is "not of this world." We are eternal beings, not just sensory flesh beings. God has to fashion us for eternity. Suffering disturbs our earthly happiness and forces us to stretch to another dimension for our strength and satisfaction. This stretching causes us to know God, who is Spirit, and ourselves created in his image as spirit beings, instead of mere flesh beings. Jesus told the woman at the well that "the true worshippers must worship Him in Spirit and truth." Yet, unless we experience some sort of detachment from this world, we would be satisfied to worship him only in safe earthly buildings filled with fantasy and falsehoods about God.

This Thing is From Me!
"Life's disappointments are veiled love's appointments."

My child, I have a message for you today; let me whisper it in your ear, that it may gild with glory any storm clouds which may arise, and smooth the rough places upon which you may have need to tread. It is short, only five words, but let them sink into your inmost soul; use them as a pillow upon which to rest your weary head. **This thing is from Me**.

Have you ever thought of it, that all that concerns you concerns Me too? For, "He that toucheth you, toucheth the apple of mine eye" (Zech. 2:8). You are very precious in My sight (Isa. 43:4). Therefore, it is My special delight to educate you.

I would have you learn when temptations assail you, and the "enemy comes in like a flood." that **this thing is from Me,** that your weakness needs My might, and your safety lies in letting Me fight for you.

Are you in difficult circumstances, surrounded by people who do not understand you, who never consult your taste, who put you in the background? **This thing is from Me**. I am the God of circumstances. Thou camest not to thy place by accident, it is the very place God meant for thee.

Have you not asked to be made humble? See then, I have placed you in the very school where this lesson is taught; your surroundings and companions are only working out My will.

Are you in money difficulties? Is it hard to make both ends meet? **This thing is from Me,** for I am your purse-bearer and would have you draw from and depend upon Me. My supplies are limitless (Phil. 4:19). I would have you prove my promises. Let it not be said of you, "In this thing ye did not believe the Lord your God" (Deut. 1:32).

Are you passing through a night of sorrow? **This thing is from Me.** I am "the man of sorrows and acquainted with grief." I have let earthly comforters fail you, that by turning to Me you may obtain everlasting consolation (2 Thess. 2:16-17). Have you longed to do some great work for Me and instead have been laid aside on a bed of pain and weakness? **This thing is from Me.** I could not get your attention in you busy days and I want to teach you some of My deepest lessons. "they also serve who only stand and wait." Some of My greatest workers are those shut out from active service, that they may learn to wield the weapon of all-prayer.

This day I place in your hand this pot of holy oil. Make use of it freely, My child. Let every circumstance that arises, every work that pains you, every interruption that would make you impatient, every revelation of your weakness be anointed with it. The sting will go as you learn **to see Me in all things.**[1]

---

1. Taken from: "Streams in the Desert" by: Mrs. C.E. Cowman. This article is written by: Laura A. Snow.

19.
Suffering is Love in Disguise

"For whom the Lord loveth he chastens, and scourges every son whom he receiveth."
(Hebrews 12:6)

Nothing in the universe happens that is not a form of God's redeeming love. Since "Christ is all and in all" (Col. 3:11) then nothing can be separated from Him and His love purposes for us. The little verse in I John 4:16, "God is Love" has a very powerful meaning: God cannot be or give anything to us that is not love. That is what makes every tragedy of life safe, for it has hidden within it God's unfathomable love. A good friend of mine, Marty Latter, once wrote, "We can only catch a glimpse of the enormity of God's love. It is too high. The finished tapestry subjects all to Him in risen glory. I praise my God, for His steadfast Love endures forever and His faithfulness to all generations." We can be sure, then, that suffering is a facet of God's ever faithful and mercifully steadfast love.

Let us look closer within ourselves to see what happens in us when we suffer. The hidden truth behind all suffering is this: it is not what happens to us that is the problem, but how we take it. A person can live behind prison bars and be gloriously free on the inside. Likewise, we can have broken bodies, yet live free, giving praise and worship to God in our spirits.

The philosopher, Soren Kierkegaard, says that all reality and truth is subjective, not objective. He says that objectivity lies to us, because it is constantly changing, while subjectivity is constant, true, and our real reality. All we really have is ourselves, and how we take what happens to us. That is why, if we are to ever get an answer to our sufferings, it must be answered in the self, our spirit center, and not pacified by a **logistic** change.

Recently there was an article in "THE RECORDER," a local newspaper produced by the Catholic church. The article was titled, "Pope recovering from broken bone." The article was reporting on the Pope's recovering after suffering a broken leg. The interesting part, to me, was in the second half of the article titled, "Pope is well acquainted with nature of suffering." I would like to quote most of what the second half says: "As he recovers from surgery to replace part of a broken right thigh bone with a metal prosthesis, Pope John Paul II might recall some of his own words and writings about the nature of suffering and its meaning to Christians. At his general audience, the day before he fell April 29th and broke his leg, the pope said, "The 'Gospel of Suffering' is written by those who suffer together with Christ, being united with him in his messianic mission."

"Accepting trials freely and with confident obedience to the Father's will, completes 'what is lacking in Christ's afflictions for the sake of his body, the church," as Pope John Paul quoted from Paul's first letter to the Corinthians.

He added that through our sufferings, believers can make a total gift of themselves to God and can reach the highest degree of love. In his message for the 1994 World Day of the Sick, he said that human suffering and sickness can be the source of loving sacrifice rather than a sign of God's punishment. "All the tribulations of life can become signs and promises of future glory."

John Paul said that it is never easy to discern the designs and love of God in one's suffering, but with the eyes of faith people can find peace and joy despite their pain. "Earthly suffering, when it is accepted in love, is like a bitter nut which encloses the seed of new life." However, his most notable discussion on suffering was a 1984 apostolic letter on suffering, in which the pope urged Christians to see their woes and pain as a way of becoming closer to God, not as some sort of retribution for sin.

"The passion of Christ is the key to an individual's understanding of why we suffer," the letter said. Christ's death brought an end to "definitive suffering" or the loss of eternal life. With Christ's sacrifice, he said, suffering "entered into a completely new dimension and a new order, for it has been linked to love."

It is easy enough for us Christians to understand why we suffered before we were born-again, because without it we would never have seen our need for Christ. We suffered because we were not right with God, and unconsciously sought for fulfillment in things, people, positions in life, money, sex, etcetera. This suffering has been coined as "a heart shape vacuum" in our hearts longing to be filled. What I like calling it is an "insatiable hunger desiring to be satisfied."

We suffer because we were created to contain the Creator, and instead, we contain the satanic nature, who silently rapes and ravishes us by expressing his nature through us in the form of sin. The result of this agony is as the Bible says, "death." "The wages of sin is death" (Romans 6:23). Ironically, without this agony we would never seek God. After all, God subjected us to this vanity, in hope of getting us back (Rom. 8:20). So God deems this suffering very necessary in the preparation and conditioning of the sinner to find his Savior.

Secondly, we see throughout the New, as well as the Old Testament, the necessity for suffering to purify and sanctify the born-again and chosen vessel. Even Jesus had his training in life through suffering, as we have already seen in Hebrews 5:8. Job is the prime example in the old Testament, "though he slay me, yet will I trust him." John the Baptist prophesied of a baptism of fire that would purify the Christian, and I Corinthians 3:13 reiterates, "Every man's work shall be made manifest: for the day shall declare it, because it shall be revealed by fire; and the fire shall try every man's work of what sort it is." In the Revelation, John brings out how we are clothed with the fine linens of righteousness: "I counsel thee to buy of me **gold tried in the fire**, that thou mayest be rich; and white raiment, that thou mayest be clothed, and that the shame of thy nakedness do not appear; and anoint thine eyes with eye-salve, that thou mayest see" (Rev. 3:18). And in John 15, Jesus teaches about the vine and the branch. There he gives us a metaphor for Christian maturity with the three different stages of pruning. We, the branch, must endure severe pruning for successful fruit bearing.

Purifying by fire is God's necessary and loving tool to condition the Christian for eternal life which begins here and now. Eternal means just that, not temporal. We are eternal beings, operating and acting as if we are just temporal flesh beings. Our natural senses have been our thermometer of reality. But now we see that our home is eternity, which is the eternal now in the Spirit. We must know how to operate the things not seen, not the things felt in our natural senses. The baptism of fire accomplishs just that.

Then thirdly, suffering is seen on the part of the intercessor, which means our suffering is for others, not ourselves. II Corinthians gives testimony to Paul's intercessory agonies, which the Bible calls "our reasonable service." II Corinthians 4:8-18 sums all this up and gives us the purposed glory behind our suffering: "We are always delivered unto death for Jesus' sake, that the life also of Jesus might be made manifest in our mortal flesh. So then death works in us, but life in others, because our outer man is perishing, but our inner man of the spirit is renewed day by day."

So if we catch the glory behind suffering, then it is a light affliction, and it works for us a far more exceeding and eternal weight of glory. We are Spirit people who worship God in the Spirit and have no confidence in flesh appearances. These appearances are only temporal and passing. As Spirit people we look at the things not seen as our reality.

Suffering is God's necessary tool to wake us up from a dream world of illusion. It shakes our natural world, which satisfies our flesh, it makes us stretch to the unseen Spirit world, which is the only reality, and it conditions us to see who we really are in Christ. This is all a healthy background that brings alive in us the real truth of Christ, who is our life. With the truth established in us, we are then equipped to, "Bear one another's burdens, and so fulfill the law of Christ" (Galatians 6:2).

20.

"The Fellowship of His Suffering"

"That I may know him, and the power of his resurrection, and the fellowship of his sufferings, being make comformable unto his death."
(Philippians 3:10)

I have shared the last part of my Mother's life in a previous chapter ("A Severe Mercy") but there is so much more. She became a Christian when she was about sixty-five. She had rheumatoid arthritis for years before her conversion. After her conversion, she attended an Assembly of God fellowship. She thought the Lord would surely heal her body. I can remember her going to every healing service in town and some out of town.

After about two years, she sought the Lord for an answer for her unhealed body. I'm so thankful that she did not condemn herself for lack of faith, like so many Christians do. Instead, she asked the Lord for His answer to her sickness. It came so clearly in her; healing has nothing to do with our temporal bodies, for they are secondary to the real healing of our spirits. The Lord wanted her to know who she really was in Christ.

She saw that the scripture in Isaiah 53, "by his stripes ye are healed," referred to the inner healing of the heart.

Total deliverance means that you know oneness with Christ. Jesus prayed that prayer in John 17, "that they might be one, even as we are one." Obviously, this was a further step in her total healing of the inner man.

She astounded her church one day at a healing service. Holding up her crippled hands, she asked ; "Look at my hands! Do you say that I am not healed because you see that they are still crippled? I tell you that the real healing is not in my hands, but in the inner man of the heart. God has given me the revelation of who I am, and now it doesn't even matter if my hands are crippled or not. Christ is pleased to live in my crippled body. It glorifies Him." What man despises, God glorifies. The Cross of Christ was like that.

One time, she went to the front for an altar call. The people were kneeling in prayer to get their needs met. She stood over them, outwardly looking like one of the most needy. Then in the power of the Holy Spirit, she demanded their attention. "Get up! You don't have any needs. If you have Jesus, he has already given you all you need, by giving you himself. So get up, you are praying a prayer of unbelief." Needless to say, they did.

Another time she went to the hospital for a hip replacement. While she was there she led a nun to the Lord by her spirit of praise. She didn't believe in defeat; she believed in God only in every situation. That is total inner healing.

All the rest of her life was an opportunity for praise. By the time she got to the "grand finale" in her life, she was like Abraham, "a friend of God." She was God's friend because she could, "call the things that be not, as though they were." I call it the "grand finale" because cancer took her life. But did it? She would have said "No! My life is not me, it's Jesus, and in Him I will never die."

She totally astounded me the day in the hospital when I had to tell her that she had cancer. She responded by saying, "We are not going to give the devil one bit of credit for this, this cancer is from God! It can't really touch me anyway, because I'm dead and resurrected in Christ. So, Sylvia don't cry for me, give glory to God and just keep on thanking and praising Jesus."

One time three ministers from her church came to lay hands on her for healing. They were all very tall compared to her 4'11" stature. She gave them a sermon that day that I will never forget, saying, "Don't lay hands on me for healing; I have cancer and I am going to die. Oh, but this cancer can't kill me, I'm already dead in Christ. When I look in the mirror I don't see Leona, I see Jesus; He is raised from the dead as me." Those three ministers were slain in the Spirit that day. They had never heard anything so powerful.

I stayed by her side day and night, because the glory of the Lord was so illuminating to me that I considered it "Holy Ground." Then at the end, the Lord gave me the greatest treasure of my life. She was in pain, so I was to be with her to give her pain shots, because my dad wasn't able to. That night she agonized in great pain all night long. I gave her shots every four hours as directed. That night I wrestled with the Lord. How could he allow her to be in so much pain when she had done nothing but praise Him all through her sickness? If this is what He was about then I wanted out: "Strike me out of the Lamb's Book of Life!"

The next morning when I went in to her, she was back to herself, and I asked her, "Mom, do you remember how much pain you were in last night?" "Nooo", she said. "Oh, Sylvia did you forget? This is not happening to me, it is happening to Jesus!" Her faith had transcended her pain!! I had forgotten, but I won't anymore. That statement has made more of an impact on my life than anything ever would. She died that day with her finger pointing up in praise to our Father who does all things well.

Would her life have made such an impact if she had gotten outer healing? I think not. People forget outer healing, but this story will never be forgotten. The word that had come to me when I found out she had cancer was from Romans 8:18: "I reckon that the sufferings of this present time are not worthy to be compared with the glory which shall be revealed in us." This word was fulfilled before my eyes in the life of my mother. Even today her "fruits do follow her," as we are seeing every thing she asked for come into being.

In John 15:16, Jesus is talking to his disciples about the new relationship of oneness with God. He said that a friend of God will bear **remaining fruit**. Remaining fruit isn't temporal deliverances of healing. Neither could it be casting out demons. We are all going to die, so outer healing could not be permanent, or the "fruit that remains." The fruit that remains has to be fruit that lasts for eternity. My Mother paid a price that God had to honor. We **might** get our prayers answered, but we **must** get what we intercede for. It reminds me of a verse in Hebrews 11:35: "not accepting deliverance, that they might obtain a better resurrection." She refused outer healing in the flesh so that there would be spiritual resurrection of oneness with God for all her people.

Before Mom died, she held up her crippled hands and counted on her fingers what she wanted from the Lord. She didn't **ask** the Lord, she took it for granted that she would get everything that she wanted: my brother inwardly healed from his earlier child abuse; my younger brother saved, my sister saved, my David restored to the Lord, my dad comforted at her death, and many other demands. But nothing for me! I wondered why.

After her death, I was tortured by the memory of her vomiting during her last hours. I hated it, then the Spirit said to me, "What did she say about herself?" I thought, then I said, "She always quoted, 'Out from **me** shall flow rivers of living water.' I replaced the horror of what I envisioned with her scripture, and it helped me. Then, two days later, the Spirit said to me, "It was through your mother's intercessory death that, now out from **you** shall flow rivers of living water!" I was totally taken back. She was a lamb **for me!** Out of her death, God was bringing resurrection in **me**. She always said, "my life is not me, it is Jesus." Jesus had come in her body and laid down his life in her, for me. I was speechless, and totally awestruck. My mother had given up her life **for me**. Only a God of great wisdom and love could turn the pain and agony my mother and I had suffered with each other into a great and wonderful love story. I am eternally grateful.

My sister Ruth died unexpectedly several years ago while we were waiting for her husband and my brother-in-law to die of cancer. Six months later, he died. Both died in the Lord, a fruit of my mother's intercession. Out of these deaths has come spiritual life for my nieces, and an open door for a Bible class in her liberal Presbyterian church. Many were brought to the Lord and to the illuminating revelation of who they are.

Every request, or should I say demand, that my mother put on the Lord, I have seen come to pass. Not one has been left out. As the scripture says, "Blessed are the dead which die in the Lord from henceforth; Yea, saith the Spirit, that they may rest from their labors; and their **works** do follow them" (Rev. 14:13).

So here I am, a fool, praising God for my mom's cancer, for my sister and brother-in-law's deaths, for my son's drug addiction, for a daughter-in-law who is a stripper, for another son's run-away wife, for my daughter's fat body, for pain, for suffering, and for God's convenient agent, Satan, whom God greatly uses for our good. All these things prove that we are "more then conquerors," and that the Cross is really our friend and not our enemy.

21.
My Uncle Bill

*"Let us offer the sacrifice of praise
to God continually, that is, the fruit of our lips
giving thanks to his name."*
(Hebrews 13:15)

    My Uncle Bill was married to my mother's sister, Irene. They had no children, so the Lord privileged me to love them as my own mother and father.
    My aunt Irene had been spiritually enlightened through my mother's death. She had never known that God lived **in** people until she experienced watching my mother die the glorious death that she did. Irene actually saw the glory of the Lord that radiated through my mother's sufferings. She said to me one day, "Sylvia, I don't see Nona lying there dying of cancer. I see Jesus lying there, turning suffering into glory." I knew that flesh and blood had not told her this glorious truth-- it was pure revelation. From that day on, I talked to her as if she knew all the same spiritual truths that I knew. Funny thing, she always rose up to what I was saying. She didn't have the words, but her spirit leaped to my words.
    Her one great pain in life was that her husband, Bill, didn't know the Lord. Uncle Bill lived his whole life professing to be an atheist. He was a racist and a bigot, and he and my aunt battled most of their 55 years of marriage, although Irene loved him dearly. Then, about two years ago, we were sitting in my living room discussing his spiritual condition, when the Lord gave me a word of faith.
    The lights turned on as I said to Irene, "Let's pray for him through a word of faith. Let's believe that Bill is **not an**

atheist! I don't care what he says with his mouth, we are going to believe that he is really a believer in his heart." Then I went on to say to her that Jesus said, "If two of you shall agree on earth as touching any thing that they shall ask, it shall be done for them of my Father which is in heaven" (Matthew 18:19). Irene and I made a pact with God that day.

Two, maybe three months later, Bill was diagnosed with colon cancer. It originated in his gall bladder. Self-sufficiency, which thinks it can handle anything, cannot handle weakness. So he began to talk about God. This was just the beginning of a long battle with the Spirit as God prepared him to receive the forgiveness of his sins which is in Christ. During that time he took all his frustrations out on my aunt. She stood strong in faith, unwavering in her word of faith for him.

Years earlier, Irene had learned through her own battle with diabetes, that self-pity would be his real enemy. It is never what happens **to** us that is the problem; it is what we **do with it** that is the solution or the real problem. Irene learned that by accepting her disease and trusting God she could learn to live with it. But if she had continued to feel sorry for herself and fight it, instead of accepting it, she would have been buried by it. She knew the same would be true for Bill, so she would never feel sorry for him or let him feel sorry for himself. She was tough, but I think that was the thing that pressed him into God, instead of self-pity.

All this was very hard on Irene, so she would comfort herself by going into the garden and feeding the birds. One of them became quite tame, helping her fill those dark days with friendship and love. I call her St. Francis of Assisi. One day she was telling me how her bird watched for her and would come down and eat from her hand. As I listened, I asked her what kind of bird it was. When she told me it was a mockingbird, I roared with laughter. "Don't you know that he has a message to you from God," I said. "What is He saying," she asked? "The mocking bird is the only bird I know of that sings at night! He is telling you to just keep singing praises to

God, no matter how dark things get. Just keep singing." And that she did. Her faith soared during those two years of nursing Bill, as she just kept on praising God.

I had no real outer evidence Uncle Bill was responding to the Spirit's call. But faith, as we know, is its own evidence and doesn't need any outer signs. But the Spirit was generous to me with a surprise word. It came while I was visiting my father in the nursing home. He has Parkinson's disease, and his mental faculties are not always clear. I usually play along with him in his imaginations, although I always listen for a message from the Spirit.

One day he said to me, "Bill came to visit me." "He did!" I said. "Yes, he told me that he loves you as much as he loves Jesus Christ!" This startled me, but it made me think. Later that day I opened my Bible and my eyes fell on a passage in the Gospels. Jesus was saying to his disciples, "He that receiveth you, receiveth me, and he that receiveth me, receiveth him that sent me" (Matthew 10:40). I took it by faith that Uncle Bill was actually receiving Christ by receiving me.

Weak as Bill was, he came to my house on Thanksgiving as usual. As he was leaving, he looked at me and said, "I'm not going to make it much longer." I looked at him and said, "Is that all right with you Uncle Bill?" "Yes," he said, "whenever the good Lord wants me." Then I said, "Do you want me to come and talk to you about that?" "Yes I do," he said.

The last two years were God's mercy, as the Spirit prepared him for eternity. God is forever loving and relentless with his pressures. He alone knows how to break a person down who is steeped in self-sufficiency. The day that I went to talk with him, he confessed all his sins to me as I shared with him the power in the cleansing blood of Christ. What a privilege it is to bring our loved ones the Good News of the Gospel. Then a precious thing happened. He asked me to speak at his funeral, saying, "I don't have a preacher you know--will you be my preacher?" It humbled me, and I said,

"Of course I will." Our simple word of faith in the mighty saving arm of God was being manifested right before my eyes. Is anything or anyone too hard for God?

On Christmas Eve, Uncle Bill died early in the morning without ever having pain. Hallelujah!! Irene has been praising the Lord continuously. She has blessed everyone who knows her. "Now thanks be unto God, which always causeth us to triumph in Christ, and maketh manifest the savor of his knowledge by us in every place" (II Cor. 2:14).

The funeral was not until Monday morning. The night before, I still had not prepared anything for the service. In the middle of the night I woke up in a sweat and started trying to put some scriptures in order. The Spirit said to me, "Go back to bed; it will come as easily as the events of any normal day." I did, and fell sound asleep. About 7:00 A.M. I woke up and began thinking about seeds.

All the power of the universe is hidden in a tiny seed. When you hold a seed in your hand, you are looking at the promise of new life hidden under its hard shell. For when you look at an acorn, you are really seeing a full grown oak tree, bearing thousands of seeds of its own.

I began the funeral by telling them that God had promised the seed, which is Christ, and that seed would be planted in every man (Gen. 3:15 & John 1:9). God is the gardener, Christ is the seed, and we are the garden. The gardener is the one who prepares the soil (by the Holy Spirit) for the growth of the seed. Then the Holy Spirit, like the hound of heaven, is relentlessly preparing the garden. Everything that comes to us, good or evil, comes to us from the loving hand of our Father, who causes all things to work together for our good. Bill's cancer was the mercy of God's preparation for new life and that new life was Christ coming to birth in him.

Uncle Bill was a Christian for only two weeks before he died. Was his life a waste? Not in God's sight. Remember, God sees an oak tree. Matthew 20:1-16 tells a story about Jesus walking along with his disciples and saying that, "The kingdom of heaven is like a man who rose early in the morning to go to the market place to find workers for his vineyard. He found workers and hired them for a penny, which was a day's wage. Later that day, at the third hour he decided he needed more workers. So he hired more laborers and told them he would give them whatever was right, and they agreed. He repeated the same thing the sixth hour, until it was the eleventh hour. He found some in the market place standing idle, and asked them, "Why are you standing idle? Go work for me and I will pay you what is right."

Now when the day's work was over, the workers came to him for their wages. The owner of the vineyard gave everyone the same wage, one penny for his work. The ones hired early in the day grumbled and said, "These men who were hired last worked only one hour. And you have made them equal to us who have borne the burden of the work and the heat of the day." But he answered them, "Friend, I am not being unfair to you. Didn't you agree to work for a penny? Take your pay and go. I want to give the man who was hired last the same as I gave you. Don't I have the right to do what I want with my own money? Or are you envious because I am generous?" "So the last shall be first, and the first last."

What is first and foremost in God's heart is the man who knows that he does not deserve to get the full wage, but gets it anyway. That man truly knows God's grace, while the others are self-righteous and falsely think they deserve and need more. That man is last in the kingdom of God.

Uncle Bill was an eleventh hour person who worked only one hour, yet received the same wage as us all. And what is the work that he did? Jesus said that the work of God is to simply believe in Him (John 6:28). What a God!

Uncle Bill's death is bearing much fruit as the promise said, "Except a corn of wheat fall into the ground and die, it remains alone, but if it dies it will bring forth much fruit" (John 12:24). The one principle and promise of the universe is that life must come out of death. Life begins in death, for

Jesus said in Matt. 16:24, "Unless you lose your life, you will not find life." What we lose is a false, independent life that agrees with Satan, "I will be like the most High God." Just think of the pride of the creature that believes that in separation he has a will of his own, and strives to be like the Creator! In our deception, we don't realize that we are really a counterfeit like Satan. For no one can be like God, apart from being God. The only way to be like God is to submit ourselves in a death to our satanic egos, filled with striving self-effort, and humbly rest in the life of Christ as us.

I will always remember the life of my precious Uncle Bill, for it represents all the lost people everywhere waiting for someone to believe the impossible for them. All the power of the universe is contained in a tiny seed, and that seed of Christ is in every man, waiting to be birthed. Let us all "laugh at impossibility and shout IT SHALL BE DONE!"

This was the faith cry declared by C.T. Studd as he made his way into the African jungles sharing Christ. His desire was to see "Jesus running around in black bodies." The fruit of his labor of faith still speaks today as a testimony to his believing in impossibilities. A mustard seed is a small thing, yet Jesus says that is all the faith we need. Can we dare to believe? For, "All things are possible to them that believe."

22.

Intercession

"For I could wish that myself were accursed from Christ for my brethren, my kinsmen according to the flesh."
(Romans 9:3)

What is an intercession? Webster's definition (an act interceding; with a prayer for mercy) pales at the great Biblical definition of intercession exemplified by our Lord, and recorded in Isaiah 53: "Surely our grief He Himself bore, and our sorrows He carried; But He was pierced for our transgressions, He was crushed for our iniquities; The chastening for our well-being fell upon Him, and by His scourging we are healed. Because He poured out Himself unto death, and was numbered with the transgressors; Yet He Himself bore the sin of many, and interceded for the transgressors."

Our heavenly Father could not bear to leave his top creation, man, in his justly deserved consequences for sin. For these consequences would mean spiritual and physical death which would eternally separate us from our maker. God's purpose from the beginning of creation was to provide himself an intercessor, for Revelation 13:8 says that Christ is "The Lamb slain from the foundation of the world." It's curious to me that this verse says that God foreknew our fallen condition and made a provision before the very first sin was ever committed.

Isa. 59:16 says that God looked for a man to stand in the gap, and found none. Therefore, He sent his only Son, the sacrificial Lamb of God, to stand in the gap and intercede for the sin of the whole world. He vicariously became what we were (sin) in order that we might be what he is (righteous).

Taking someone else's place in order to gain their freedom is the simplest definition of intercession. The very nature of God is sacrificial, for Jesus is called, "The Lamb of God" by John the Baptist. Just think, almighty God is called a **lamb**. A lamb is one of the most helpless and defenseless animals that I know of, yet God is called a lamb. This speaks loudly of the very nature of God--He would go to hell, willingly taking our place, in order to gain restoration and freedom for His creation.

This is the Divine Nature that Peter speaks about in his second epistle, "whereby are given unto us exceeding great and precious promises: that by these (promises) you might be partakers of the **Divine Nature**" (II Peter 1:4). This Nature is Christ himself living His life in and through us. This nature produces in us wisdom, righteousness, sanctification, and redemption, for it is Christ himself. This is the very oneness Paul experienced at the end of Romans Eight, "Who shall separate us from the love of Christ? Shall tribulation, or distress, or persecution, or famine, or nakedness, or peril, or sword? As it is written, For thy sake we are killed all the day long; we are accounted as sheep for the slaughter. Nay, in all these things we are more than conquerors through him that loved us. For I am persuaded, that nothing shall be able to separate us from the love of God, which is in Christ Jesus our Lord."

It is very interesting to me that in Chapter Nine of Romans Paul immediately turns his attention to the needs of others, namely his brothers the Jews. Just listen to him, "I have great heaviness and continual sorrow in my heart. For I could wish that I myself were accursed from Christ for my brethren, my kinsmen according to the flesh." He had just said in chapter eight that nothing could separate him from Christ, yet now he is crying out for hell if it would save his kinsmen. That is the very nature of God, that is the heart cry of God himself--to hell with me, to gain the liberation for other people. Now that is the very same nature that God has implanted in us as co-heirs with Christ.

I want to share a precious story which I feel illustrates what Paul meant in the great intercessory declaration of Romans 9:3, "I wish that myself were accursed from Christ for my brethren's sake."

My son-in-law, Daniel, reminds me of David the shepherd boy who Samuel anointed with oil that day in Jesse's house. David was the least of Jesse's sons, and when the man of God came to anoint a King, Jesse didn't even think of his youngest son, David, who was just a young unnoticed shepherd boy obediently tending the sheep. Samuel's spirit didn't witness with the other brothers, who were obviously older and stronger. "No, not these, do you have another son?" Hesitantly, Jesse said, "Yes, but he is out in the field." "Get him," Samuel ordered. The Lord had given Samuel specific orders: "Look not on their countenance, or on the height of their stature; because I have refused them: for the LORD seeth not as man seeth; for man looketh on the outward appearance, but the LORD looketh on the heart" (I Samuel 16:7). I, like Jesse, was hesitant about Daniel.

Daniel is the youngest of two older brothers and two sisters. His father, who is very rich and successful, disregards him and considers him the least likely to ever be successful in his own right. Unlike his tyrannical father, Daniel is not business or money minded. His heart and mind are purely stayed only on the Lord. He is a man of the field, and if you would see him, you would have to look under the mud and grass stains to even catch his spirit.

When my daughter, Diane, wanted to marry him, I was not too sure. Not only was he unkempt, he was, I thought, a little bit crazy. That left me to find my peace from the Lord-- seeing that Diane was totally committed to marrying him. One day as he was standing by my kitchen sink talking, I supernaturally caught the light of the Spirit anointing his head. The Lord was saying to me that Daniel was his man, and I was not to go against what God had ordained. He has since become like a precious son to me.

I wanted to give to you some background on my Daniel, for God has surely anointed him, like David of old, with unconditional love. One day he was driving downtown to pick up some parts for his sister's furnace. The parts house was in the ghetto area of Louisville and as he was driving downtown, he saw a small girl. She was dirty, and crying because her mother was yanking her by the arm. Right away Daniel's heart went out to the child. The next day he went down the same street just to see if he could see her again. This time he noticed a black eye and bruises on her legs and arms. Immediately he wondered if she had been beaten. Then the question came, "Why doesn't God do something about this?" He left that day in despair. A week or two went by, and his dad sent him back downtown to the parts house. Daniel was determined to find the little girl again, as he drove down the same street.

As he passed the line of project type, ghetto houses, he saw her sitting on the porch by her fat, dirty looking, supposed mother. Next to her was a dirty old drunk man, hunched down and leaning against a wall. The little girl had a numb look on her face. She was non-respondent from abuse and neglect. Daniel's heart filled with compassion as he went around the block again, just to catch her eye. As he passed, she did look up for just a moment at him, as he smiled, but then she looked back down in desperation.

Daniel's heart cried out to God for answers as he went on, in grief, to the parts store. "How can God allow such suffering? I can understand it for the guilty, but not for little children, they are so innocent! If she had a better place to live and loving parents, that would help. But even that is only temporary. She needs to know God, but how will she know? Who will tell her? What can *I* do? I could find out where the nearest mission is and volunteer there, in hopes that she would come some day. But it all seems so hopeless!"

By the time he got near his home, there was a great storm brewing in the clouds overhead, but not nearly so powerful as the storm that was about to explode inside him. He pulled onto a dirt road and was now trembling as he cried out to God. "It's O.K. that she doesn't have any toys, and it's O.K. that she doesn't have a back yard to play in--it's even O.K. that she is poor. It's all right that her father and mother don't love her, and its even O.K. that she doesn't have a friend in the world. But God, it's **not** O.K. that she doesn't have **You**. Why can't you have the decency to give her the hope of knowing You? What kind of a God would say "Have faith", and give her nothing to *have faith* in? What kind of God would say "Have hope", and give her nothing to *hope* for?

"So if this is the way it is going to be, then take **my** back yard, take **my** money, take **my** home, take **my** family, take **my** child. Yes, even take away **my** oneness with Christ. Because if this is the way it is going to be, then take what I hold dearest. Take my salvation! Because if she can't have you, then I don't want you!"

At that moment a great tormenting darkness came on Daniel. As far as he knew, he had lost his salvation. Even in the worst darkness there is a seed of belief that God is there, but in this darkness, he experienced total hopelessness and separation from God. He said he knew that there was a God, but he was separated from him, and that, to Daniel is Hell, and total blackness. Days went by with darkness flooding his soul. At one point he stopped right in the middle of a major highway in his truck because he couldn't even push the accelerator down.

I was out of town, so I didn't know what had happened to him. While I was gone, he was in such desperation that he called me trying to tell me what had happened, but he couldn't talk about it. My spirit was immediately burdened with prayer for him, but I had no idea what had happened.

A week went by and I came back home, but I thought that I would wait for Daniel to approach me as to what his problem was. Tuesday night I went to Bible study, and on the way home I decided to go to their house. I went in and Daniel was getting ready to get into the shower. I could tell that he didn't want to talk to me, for he couldn't even look at me. I went into the next room to visit Diane and my granddaughter, Rebekah. Later he came into the room looking very distraught with a Bible in his hand.

"What are you looking for?" I asked.

"Carol (our friend) told me something about Moses and Paul, but I can't find it." Daniel has very little Bible knowledge so I tried to help him. Just off the top of my head I said to him, "Is it where Moses and Paul both said that they would give up their salvation for their brothers?" "What?" he exclaimed.

"Yes, it's here in Romans 9:3 and somewhere in the Old Testament." Then I looked at him and said, "Daniel, that **is** Jesus, you know, for the nature of God is to give up heaven and take on hell for other people." He stared at me wide eyed, but said nothing. In his mind he was thinking, "Is this right? Did these men of God really experience the same thing that I did?"

Two days later, he burst into my house with glory on his face.

"Sit down," he demanded. "You don't know what you said the other night, do you?"

"No," I replied, with uncertainty.

"You said 'Wanting to give up our salvation **is** Jesus.' That set me free, because I thought that I had lost my salvation. God brought my soul out of hell and now I know without any shadow of doubt that the little girl will know. She will know God! I'm not even as sure of my own salvation as I am sure that she will know God and His love for her.

"I paid the price of intercession. I went to hell **for her**. Nothing in life has any meaning unless God uses us in this way. Giving up our life for others **is** the meaning of life, isn't it?"

I couldn't add one more thing to that statement. For truly that is the meaning of life and it exemplifies what Jesus said in John 15:13, "Greater love hath no man than this, that a man lay down his life for his friends." Christ in Daniel's form had come to do what David had cried out in the Psalms, "For he shall deliver the needy when he crieth; the poor also, and him that hath no helper"(72:12).

Later Daniel said to me, "Sylvia, how is it that I can look at my feet and say, 'Feet move,' and they move? Then I can look at my hands and say, 'hands move,' and they move? Where does this voice come from that is talking to you now? What is this consciousness I have? Can any of us explain consciousness? Who, in the world, **am I**?

"Maybe, just maybe, God is so far away that He really is not worth knowing or having as a God, or maybe he is so close, so very close, that we can't see him, or don't recognize him **as** our feet, hands or voice. And maybe, just maybe, if he is that close, then he is going through exactly what we are going through. Just maybe, He is much more **us** than we know."

How does Daniel know all this since he is not a Bible student? He has never heard of the statement that Jesus made in John 17:21 which says, "that they may all be one; even as Thou, Father, art in Me, and I in Thee, that they also may be in Us; And the glory which Thou hast given Me I have given to them; that they may be one, just as We are one; I in them, and Thou in Me, that they may be perfected in unity". Yet amazingly Daniel is illuminated by the Spirit.

Two years later the Lord gave the final answer to Daniel's heart cry concerning the little girl's dilemma: "Daniel, now I want to tell you what kind of God I am. I am the kind of God who loves the world so much that I would give **you** to that darkness as a living sacrifice, for through death, life would come to the little girl, and the resurrected light of sonship would be birthed in you. Her great need drew my solution out of you. I am in the little girl, as well as in you. You **both** are living sacrifices in my eyes. She paid a price for you, and you paid a price for her. Her great need was necessary, for it called forth the Cross in you, that the resurrected power of the Cross in you would then loose the power of darkness in her, and that whole experience would then birth into your consciousness the true meaning of sonship.

"Now, Daniel, do you see what kind of God I am?" (John 3:16).

God is no respecter of persons--Daniel's **one** little girl, and Paul's **many** membered Jewish nation. The one is as important as the many. Nothing is too small and nothing is too big to be embraced by God's unfathomable love.

Like Daniel, we are yet in agony. For we, with God, wait for the manifestation of many sons of God coming to their glorious freedom. With our own completion in Christ secured, our hearts are turned to the needs of others. "Lord, what about my wife or husband, my children, my fellow workers, my neighbors?" Our unceasing desire is that all must know!

23.
God's Love Can Move Mountains

"For verily I say unto you, that whosoever shall <u>say</u> unto this mountain, Be thou removed and be cast into the sea, and shall not doubt in his heart, but shall believe that those things which he saith shall come to pass; he shall <u>have</u> whatsoever he <u>says</u>."
(Mark 11:23)

    I have a very precious friend that I have known for over twenty years. I first met her at a conference in Louisville in 1974. I was just barely coming out of my "great depression," and was still very socially uncomfortable, so I attached myself to the most comforting person that I could find. My friend certainly fit the bill, for being with her is like being comforted with the "balm of Gilead." After she told me about herself and her own "dark night of the soul," I considered her an expert on the subject. I asked her, "Will I have to go into anymore darknesses,' or is it over?" She looked at me with such assuring strength and said, "No, it's over." It was straight from God's mouth. And, she was right. I had little mini darknesses, but my great tribulation was over. She and I have been close friends ever since. Her great peace and love transmits to others and, I believe, transforms everyone she meets.

In the past several years she has been through an intercession in her marriage. As we have walked through it together, her great faith and the power of her "word of faith" has blessed me greatly. I have asked her to share her story in this chapter, although she wishes to remain anonymous. Here is her story.

~~~~~~~~~~

I was raised in a lovely Christian home. The whole community revered my parents as pillars of faith, as well as loving and charitable neighbors. Even though I had a good upbringing, I still hated myself and wished somehow I could be different. I believe some of my self hatred came from the fact that my upbringing was somewhat regimented in all its proper religious forms which I could never really live up to. Yet, our lives are all purposed according to God's perfect design.

After graduating from a Baptist University, I accepted a teaching position in a small town and soon met the man who was to become my husband. We married two years later. Within six years I had three children. My life was demanding, boring, and definitely not going according to my well thought-out plans. I could not get inner satisfaction or make my life work. All I wanted was to be a good Christian, a loving mother, and a wonderful wife to my husband...but I was failing miserably at all three. I was filled with guilt and inadequacies, and my frustrations caused me to yell at my children and constantly blame my husband for my discontentment and unhappiness.

God, in His loving mercy, had **meant me to fail.** He was showing me that the only answer was to know Him. Only He could fill the void in my heart. I thank God that I learned that at a young age, because it was then that I sought God in earnest. I began to associate myself with born again

Christians and discovered that Jesus was real and that He lived inside me. At last my spiritual journey had begun.

Things seemed fine for a while. I could manage to get through the difficulties with God's help, but the great void inside me which was only partially satisfied was starting to eat away at me again, and I was not at peace. So in my own way, and as much as I knew how, I gave myself to God and asked Him to take over. I was not prepared for what came next. God took me at my word and put me in great darkness just as He had done Abraham. Genesis 15:12b, "And, lo, an horror of great darkness fell upon him."

I thought I was losing my mind and no one had answers for me...not my minister, not my family, not even my born-again Christian friends. Finally, God led me to a Christian conference and one of the speakers gave an explanation that spoke to my heart. No, I wasn't losing my mind, God was settling me into Himself and He was taking me His perfect way.

Not only was the speaker's message speaking right to my heart, but he had been a missionary to the Belgian Congo in Africa. That was amazing to me, for I had always wanted to be a missionary to the Belgian Congo. So I invited him to my home town. He began to teach me truths that I had never heard in my Christian environment. He taught me how to love myself, because he taught me who I really was. He began to tell me that I was real, and that I had validity, and that I had integrity. I had never known any of this before. My missionary friend took away all the doctrine I had thought I had to have, and all the rules and all the regulations. What he said was, "You have a Person in you and that's all you need." He didn't tell me what I had to do and what I didn't have to do. All he said was "You just listen to the inner Person inside you", and that's what I've been doing ever since. I didn't realize it at the time, but God was preparing me for the next dark chapter in my life.

When we become Christians and learn the truth, we learn that we are faith people. Then God makes us **prove** it.

He makes us show Him and also prove to ourselves that we are faith people. Several years ago, my husband of 37 years decided he had had enough. I had stood in faith for him for years. Our marriage was tough from the very beginning, but we had three children, and I was going to stick it out because I believed in marriage. I believed once you made a covenant before God and before man, you are in your marriage for life. No matter what happened in my marriage, I wasn't going to leave even though there were many times that it was really hard. I thank God for His keeping power, because if that hadn't been instilled in me by Him, I would have left long ago.

On the surface, our marriage looked pretty normal. But below the surface was a different story. I spent many lonely days and week-ends while my husband excluded me from most of his activities. We lived our little pretend lives, with most of my time spent trying to satisfy him the best I could, while he was always leaving on another trip. During those lonely years, I learned how to see God in all my life's circumstances. I am eternally thankful to God, as well as my husband, for those years, because I learned invaluable lessons of seeing God only. Those were my school days. But, what about my husband? My heart's cry for my husband was to know God, and know who he really was in Christ.

Then one day God started leading me to do something that I had never done in our marriage. What He asked me to do went directly against my husband's wishes. God was asking me to build a new room on our house. This, you see, would be an embarrassment to my husband, because he was a builder. He didn't want it, nor would he build it. So I contracted another builder to do the job. I knew that doing this would be risky, but God was leading me, so I did it in the courage of the Lord.

He was furious and right away he decided to leave, but as I found out later, he was planning to leave anyway and used the new room as an excuse. For a month I thought it was my fault. Then I found out about his indiscretions, and all the gaps that were unfilled began to fill up, and all the unanswered questions were answered in about 5 seconds time. I realized that he had lead a double life for 20 years or more. I had had my suspicions, but I was so naive and so trusting I never followed them through to find out if they were really true or not.

I had an anonymous phone call in the early 70's which suggested unfaithfulness. After the call I sat on the side of the bed and said, "God, if it's true, I forgive him this time and for any other time that it has happened." God made me put my money where my mouth was and walk that out this past year. One day the girl who does my hair said, "If he comes back can you forgive him?" I said "I already have. He's already forgiven." How could I not forgive him when Jesus Christ has forgiven me? We must forgive, and it isn't our forgiveness either. It's the life of Christ in us forgiving others.

When I found out about his double life, I went to his office and threw a fit. He rightly described me as cussing like a sailor, and I did. I slammed doors and did all the things I hadn't done through the years and probably should have. But I ended by telling him who he was. I said, "That's not who you are, you're really Jesus Christ in your form." And every time I said it, he would turn his head because he had tears in his eyes.

I told him, "There is no way I can ever stop loving you because it's God's love. I don't care what you've done, it's God's love that keeps on pouring out through me to you." Of course I was in agony and experienced groanings that cannot be uttered. Just because you are a faith person, doesn't mean that you won't have agony. The agony is God's pressure to put passion into your faith, because believing is your only release. I stood on a promise in I Cor. 13:8 which says, **"Love never fails."** I love that, because it says that God's love never fails, for it cannot fail. Love and forgiveness looks like the weak way, but in fact it is the most powerful, because as God says, "It can never fail."

I would often get away and visit with Sylvia. It was during one of those visits that God gave me my word of faith. It was this: **He is coming home for Christ's sake.** I simply stood in faith and exercised my authority of faith as Mark 11:23 says, "You **shall** have whatsoever you **say**." Now I don't want him home until God does His work in him, and God is doing that work. What I believe as already eternally done, is being worked out in time and is in the process of being done in him.

Did you know that "the unbelieving husband is sanctified by the wife" (I Cor. 7:14)? My husband cannot have faith for himself, but I can stand in the gap and have faith for him. I am believing that he is "dead to sin, and alive to righteousness." I believed that he was really God's man and that he would come home, not for my sake, but for Christ's sake.

I began to tell him so. I told him that he was cleansed from sin and that he was already freed from the things that had trapped him. I told him that I knew it, and God knows it, and he would know it too, real soon. You see, faith is saying to the mountain that you see a plain even before the plain appears.

God's love is so great. It will never let people go. God loves my husband so much that He would cause me to spend a lifetime believing for him. Yes, I have spent lonely years, but I wouldn't have it any other way. It was all worth it. If it were possible, I would even spend another life time waiting and believing for him. That is how unstoppable God's love is.

One time when I was particularly low, the Lord gave me these verses from II Chronicles 20:15-17. It was when Jehoshaphat, the King of Judah, was being invaded by the Moabs. He was very afraid, but he knew who to turn to for his answer. When he asked the Lord for guidance the Lord said this to him: "Thus saith the Lord unto you, be not afraid nor dismayed by reason of this great multitude; for **the battle is not yours, but God's. Ye shall not need to fight this battle; set yourselves, stand ye still, and see the salvation of the**

Lord. Fear not, nor be dismayed; tomorrow go out against them; for the Lord will be with you."

This spoke right to my heart. The battle that I was fighting was too big and too overwhelming for me. Not only was my husband gone, but our family was divided in its response to the separation. God continually took the responsibility of resolving the situation from me, and caused me to rest in him. Now all I had to do was to let the Lord do the fighting, and I could just stand still and watch God. That is exactly what I did.

I stood still and said "my word." I said it when I was encouraged, I said it when I was discouraged. I told my friends in the community, "He **is** coming home, just watch and see." Three wonderful friends and my precious daughter stood with me. The rest were unbelieving skeptics. That did not matter, for I was firmly planted on God's promise of Mark 11:23, "That whosoever shall say unto this mountain, be thou removed, and be thou cast into the sea; and shall not doubt in his heart, but shall believe that those things which he saith shall come to pass; **he shall have whatsoever he saith**."

As I was going through this time of intercession, I read everything I could find on it. I read every chapter my missionary friend had written on it, and I also read the Bible. But I think the book that helped the most and the one I read the most was Doris Rusco's book on intercession. In it she says that intercession is a walk the **Holy Spirit** takes you through. You could not go through it by your own efforts, for it is the Holy Spirit Himself laying his life down in you for the other person.

You never come out of an intercession the way you go into it. You are a different person. Intercession is primarily for someone else, and secondarily for the intercessor. So God had to do a cleansing work in me and I say again, He **had** to, because I couldn't be a clear channel until He first cleansed me. Then His Word and His Spirit could go through into the situation and for the persons for whom I was interceding.

It hurts me to see my husband, so I purpose not to. But God has had other plans. I can't tell you how many times I see him at an intersection or getting out of his car at the office. And God told me that the purpose for this is that every time I see him, I am to say, "There goes Christ in my husband's form." And I do say it, over and over and over. And he is coming home, and he is going to know what I know, because he is God's man.

All these months God was quietly working behind the scenes in my husband's heart. Fourteen months after my husband walked out and was headed head-strong into a divorce, God changed his heart and caused him to want to come home. I was excited, but apprehensive at the same time. Was this right? Only God could show me if it was the right time.

Six months passed--it was important not to let my husband come home until I got my release from the Lord. During that time, God was doing an all important work in my husband's heart. Finally the glorious day came when the Lord gave me the long awaited release. It was time for his homecoming. God had fulfilled His promise to me and brought into being His own word of faith, which He had given me months earlier. This battle was too hard for me. But I, like King Jehoshaphat, put my trust in the living God, and it was not too hard for Him. I am constantly rejoicing and thanking the Lord for His faithfulness for He has caused my husband to return home a new man. He has truly **"come home for Christ's sake."**

24.
Kings and Priests

"You are a chosen generation, a royal priesthood, an holy nation, a peculiar people; that you should show forth the praises of him who hath called you out of darkness into His marvellous light."
(I Peter 2:9)

We are united with God in his one world purpose, which is to bring His precious creation, man, back into the pure harmony of the Garden of Eden glory. He subjected us unto vanity (Romans 8:20) hoping to train us in what isn't the truth, to then deliver us from this vanity through the Cross of Christ, and now cause us to know our deliverance and glorious liberation. So we, as co-saviors and co-creators, have the same heart that God has, which is always and eternally for others.

I think that most of us Christians have grossly missed what it means to be a minister of the Lord. **Suffering**, not prosperity, is the true hall mark of a minister, for "if we suffer with Christ, we will reign with him" (II Tim. 2:12). II Corthinians 6:4-10 brings us clarity on the credentials of a true minister of God. We are approved as ministers of God "in much patience, in afflictions, in necessities, in distresses, in stripes, in imprisonments, in tumults, in labours, in watchings, in fastings; by pureness, by knowledge, by longsuffering, by kindness, by the Holy Ghost, by love unfeigned, by the word of truth, by the power of God, by the armour of righteousness on the right hand and on the left, by honour and dishonour, by evil report and good report: as deceivers, and yet true;

As unknown, and yet well known; as dying, and, behold, we live; as chastened, and not killed; As sorrowful, yet alway rejoicing; as poor, yet making many rich; as having nothing, and yet possessing all things." In all these things, we are more than conquerors, while He always causes us to triumph in Christ.

Glory comes out of the suffering the same way that the light comes out of darkness, II Corinthians 4:6. That is why as sons, not children, we are not delivered from trials and temptation (James 1:3) but delivered **unto** them. For by doing so we can take on the sufferings of others as co-saviours and co-creators with God. Peter calls us "royal priests" in 1 Peter 2:9: "But ye are a chosen generation, a **royal priesthood**, an holy nation, a peculiar people; that ye should show forth the praises of him who hath called you out of darkness into his marvelous light".

We are called "royal" because as Kings we reign with Christ far above all principality, and power, and might, and dominion, for the devil and all his evil forces are already under the feet of Jesus, even though we don't see it yet (Heb.2:8b). We know for ourselves the "power of his resurrection" and have the "keys of the kingdom." With this knowing, we dare break the bondage that chains our brothers and sisters to lies and false identities. We do this by speaking "the word." Jesus said, "**Say** unto that mountain be thou removed and cast into the sea, for you shall have whatsoever you **say**. Therefore I say unto you, What things so ever ye desire, when you pray, **believe** that ye receive them, and ye **shall** have them" (Mark 11:23).

We are also called "priests" because we present our bodies as living sacrifices, and doing so is our reasonable service. That simply means that we give ourselves to our negative crosses, instead of fighting them. Our bodies don't belong to us, they belong to Christ. "You are bought with a price." There is a rest that comes when you finally accept your situation as from the Lord and as "the Father's cup." For by doing this we enter into what God's eternal purposes are for others.

We cannot experience suffering without its positive counterpart, glory. "Always causing us to triumph" (2:14); "Suffering can not be compared with the **glory**" (Rom. 8:18); "Our light afflictions worketh for us a far more exceeding and eternal weight of **glory**" (II Cor. 4:18). Suffering and glory are different forms of the same thing, like a pencil has a point on one end and an eraser on the other. They are opposite ends of the same thing. So the life of Christ manifests himself in opposite but unified forms: a sacrificial lamb, a conquering lion, and they both rest together as harmonious friends. The prophetic scripture is fulfilled, "The lion will lie down with the lamb."

We all have one ministry and that is "the ministry of reconciliation" (II Cor. 5:18). None of us can fully rest until the whole body of Christ comes into "the unity of the faith, and of the knowledge of the Son of God, unto a perfect man, unto the measure of the stature of the fullness of Christ. From whom the whole body fitly joined together and compacted by that which every joint supplieth, according to the effectual working in the measure of every part, maketh increase of the body unto the edifying of itself in love" (Eph. 4:13 & 16).

The battle is already won in Christ. The Ephesian (6:14) warriors battle cry is to simply stand by faith and in the truth of who we really are. Jesus in us doesn't have to fight evil, he has already defeated Satan. When we know the secret of Christ suffering **as us**, we see all suffering as, "a light affliction which is for a moment, working in us a far more exceeding and eternal weight of glory. For we look not at the things which are seen, but at things which are not seen; for the things which are seen are temporal; but the things which are not seen are eternal." We Christians spend all our time trying to get **outer** deliverances and miss the true **spiritual** deliverances for our loved ones, that comes by the privilege of laying down our lives for others.

I want to end this chapter with this powerful letter that was written by Margo Sanders, my good friend:

"We are kings and priests (Rev 1:6). "And (He) hath made us kings and priests unto God" We have been given the POWER to COMMAND' (Isa 45:11)! "Thus saith the LORD, the Holy One of Israel, and his Maker, Ask me of things to come concerning my sons, and concerning the work of my hands command ye me."

So we do not blandly, fatalistically say "'Well, God's will.'" Of course God's will shall be done but we are to be involved with God's will.

Remember how Moses changed God's mind (Ex 32:9)? "And the LORD said unto Moses, I have seen this people, and, behold, it is a stiff-necked people: Now therefore let me alone, that my wrath may wax hot against them, and that I may consume them: and I will make of thee a great nation. And Moses besought the LORD his God, and said, 'LORD, why doth thy wrath wax hot against thy people, which thou hast brought forth out of the land of Egypt with great power, and with a mighty hand? Turn from thy fierce wrath, and repent of this evil against thy people. Remember Abraham, Isaac, and Israel, thy servants, to whom thou swore by thine own self, and saidst unto them, I will multiply your seed as the stars of heaven, and all this land that I have spoken of will I give unto your seed, and they shall inherit it for ever.' (Ex 32:14) 'And the LORD repented (changed his mind) of the evil which he thought to do unto his people."

Do you remember Jacob wrestling with God? (Gen 32:24) "And Jacob was left alone; and there wrestled a man with him until the breaking of the day. And when he saw that he prevailed not against him, he touched the hollow of his thigh; and the hollow of Jacob's thigh was out of joint, as he wrestled with him. And he said, "Let me go, for the day breaketh." And he said, "I will not let thee go, except thou bless me." And he said unto him, "What is thy name?" And he said, "Jacob." And he said, "Thy name shall be called no more Jacob, but Israel: for as a prince hast thou power with God and with men, and hast prevailed" (Gen 32:28).

When we burn with God's desire, we speak the word and it is finished. We may not see the outer manifestation, we may suffer for and with those we have prayed for, but we rest in faith even as our flesh carries the agonies of the person God has given us. The sufferings that we willingly take upon ourselves are a part of our royal priesthood. We intercede, we carry people, we suffer with them, we die with them, and we resurrect with them.

We are not called to be observing, detached bystanders. We are active, faithful participants, in God's will, counting ourselves as sheep for the slaughter, just as Christ was a Lamb for slaughter. Death works in us so that we may call forth Life for others (2 Cor 4:12).

The final death in us is that we have died to our own independent-self and been resurrected in Christ and newness of life.

Are we willing to die again, and again and again and again ... for others, so that they may know what we have been privileged to know? Will we give ourselves over to bondage once again in order to set another free? We must go into their hell in order to rescue them. The cost is tremendous, but so is the final victory! We hold the keys to the kingdom. We can bind people up (when they need to be bound) and we can set them free.

Rom 8:16 says, "The Spirit itself beareth witness with our spirit, that we are the children of God: And if children, then heirs; heirs of God, and joint-heirs with Christ; if so be that we suffer with him, that we may be also glorified together. For I reckon that the sufferings of this present time are not worthy to be compared with the glory which shall be revealed in us' (Rom 8:19). 'For the earnest expectation of the creature waiteth for the manifestation of the sons of God." And so I spoke: "Come forth." And I paid a price. Now it is your time to call forth life out of death.

25.
Prisoners of Hope

"Turn you to the stronghold, ye prisoners of hope, even today do I declare that I will render double unto thee;"
(Zechariah 9:12)

    I want to share with you some of my own, personal faith ventures. For if all of what I have shared so far were only theory, taught to me by my Bible teachers, then I would be speaking to you out of head knowledge instead of out of what is real in my own life experiences. Let me start with my son David, for our children are probably the thing that the Lord uses most to teach us faith.

    David became a Christian at the age of ten. Christ was so real to him that he voluntarily went before our church and gave his testimony. "I have been a sinner for ten years, but now I have received Jesus, and he has forgiven me of all my sins." It was quite a bold testimony for a ten year old! At thirteen years of age the kids on our street were calling him "preacher," because he was preaching the gospel to his friends. It was amazing, because some of them became saved.

    At the end of high school he had lost his first love and was desperately searching for himself. David has always been the most insecure of all my children, and everything he tried always seemed to fail. His self esteem was very low and that is probably why he was always trying so hard to impress people. He went to the Navy at seventeen, found it too demanding, and faked sleep walking in order to get discharged. He found himself going from job to job and finally ended up as a truck driver. By this time he was on heavy drugs. He told me later that he was snorting cocaine, smoking marijuana, taking Quaaludes, tripping on acid and drinking heavily. What desperate people will do to drown out their miseries!

There would be months that would go by when I didn't know where he was. I learned how to trust in the unseen by simply putting my trust in my Father who does all things well. On one occasion I was disheartened when I heard his favorite song on the radio. "Lord can I ask you for just one thing," I said. "Could you let me know if he is dead or alive?" A few hours later my other son, Danny, came in and threw the mail on my kitchen counter. There among the letters was a citation from California addressed to David. As I opened it, the Lord said to me, "See, he is alive and in my hands."

Later on he returned home announcing his marriage to a girl, who, I found out later, was a stripper. When Heather came into my life, I wondered if she had come from outer space. I didn't know anyone on this planet thought the way she did, for I had never been around a person with a street mentality. She would probably be diagnosed as a sociopath. Lying was such a way of life for her that she didn't even know the difference between the truth and a lie and didn't care. When I first met her, she was pregnant and married, but not to the father of her unborn child, and she was wanting to date my son. She thought this was all normal. I will never forget the night David called to tell me that he and Heather were married. I said to him, "I am so sorry, I didn't want you to, but I will have to say that God means this marriage for good." I wrestled with God for months with that one.

Finally the Lord broke me as I was reading the simple verse, John 3:16. Heather was no different from anyone else in the world without Christ, and God so loved the world that He gave his only begotten son to be crucified. And since I was Christ in my form, I loved her that much too, and I too could give my son to her. God had turned the hate in me into self-giving love--such love that at one point after I claimed her for the Lord, I told God that I would go to hell before I would see her there.

David was getting worse and worse: more drugs, more sad stories to tell me, and more and more distant from the God of his childhood. The more I did for him the worse he got. Then the day came when the Lord told me to give him over to the devil: " Do nothing more for him outwardly." By the grace of God, I knew I had to turn my back on him.

The next day, he was in an explosion that put him in the hospital and he was almost killed. I went to see him but the word came to me from the Lord to do nothing, not even to go back to the hospital. So I turned my back on him that day, knowing I was turning him over to the devil. But was it the devil? No, I knew Christ, Mr. Resurrection, was really in him, and God could not leave his son in hell. God would bring him out of hell His way, and I was not to touch it. Was I not seeing evil any more? You bet! That is what got me through. If I had spent my time fighting and rebuking Satan, I would have missed the glory of the present tense Deliverer who works all things after the counsel of His will. Also, it would have concentrated my whole thinking on the problem instead of the solution.

Remember the Old Testament story in Numbers 21:5-9. It is the one where the children of Israel disobeyed and the Lord sent the judgment of the venomous serpents to bite them. But look at the remedy the Lord provided. Moses made a fiery brass serpent and put it on a pole. When they were bitten by the serpent, they were to look at the pole and live. To look down at the serpent's bite was to die, but looking up at the pole was to be saved.

If I looked down at David's circumstances and the serpent who appeared to have him in bondage, the devil, I would have died. No, it was looking up at the serpent on the pole that saved me. Isn't that what it means to not see evil any more? In fact in John 3:14-15, Jesus likens himself on the Cross to that serpent on the pole. Don't we conquer evil in the same way Jesus did, by dying to it? We die to the false power it appears to have and rise to the operation of the faith of God, who overcame the power of death by raising Jesus from the dead. Hell has no power; death has no sting. Jesus rendered Satan powerless at Calvary, and he only has the false power **we** give him by believing in his bluffs.

A year went by, and suddenly David appeared one day. By his words he tried to convince me that he was better, but my heart told me it was another trick to try to make me feel sorry for him and help him, which I refused to do. I said to the Lord, "He's only half cooked! I don't want him back until he's fully cooked. Send him back into the fire!"

Then after two years, he appeared on my door step a broken man, so broken that the Lord said to me, "Take him in; you can help him now." Just two weeks earlier the Lord had given me a verse from Zechariah (9:12), "Turn you to the strong hold **ye prisoners of hope**, even today do I declare that I will render double unto thee." That is exactly what I was, a prisoner of hope, and this was my promise for David **and** for Heather, for they both were my double portion.

I spent months counseling with him as he poured out his deepest heart to me. Months went by before I could get him within hearing distance of the truth of God, so I gave him no spiritual answers, I just listened. Then one night around three in the morning, sitting in my kitchen, he looked at a plaque on my wall which had a verse from Galatians (2:20).

Tears poured down his face as he identified with Christ on the Cross dying **as** him. That old David was dead, and the one living in him was really Christ. **This** was the identity he had been searching for all of his life. He was really Christ in his David form. His form was created right and was acceptable to God just like it was. He didn't have to do anything but just believe. How could he do anything else at that point? His whole life had been the necessary background to bring him to this place of revelation.

I was seeing the fulfillment of a pact I had made with God years ago when my children were small. I told God that I did not want my children to be adults who just sat on church benches, going through the motions of Christianity and being numb to God. I wanted them to really know God in the same way I knew God, and I knew the hell it would take to condition them to know. It took ten years on drugs, a divorce, and lots of anguish and hell to bring David to that point. I say with God that in no other way could he have seen, but to walk through the fires of hell and be rescued by the inner resurrection of the Spirit. I praise God for every hellish minute and bow my knee to the one who set David's life in motion and charted the path for him to take.

Psalms 139 sums up David's life best: "Thou hast beset me behind and before, and laid thine hand upon me. Such knowledge is too wonderful for me; it is high, I cannot attain unto it. Whither shall I go from thy spirit? Or whither shall I flee from thy presence? If I ascend up into heaven, thou art there: if I make my bed in hell, behold thou art there. For thou hast possessed my reins; thou hast covered me in my mother's womb."

Today, David is a restored man who really knows who he is. The Lord has given him a precious Christian wife, Susan, and a completely new life. It is wonderful to see my son restored outwardly, but I am really blessed by what he sees on the inside, and that could only come through hell.

One day he said to me, "Mom, I used to think I didn't know how anyone could get through the day without being stoned, now I don't know how anyone can get though the day without the Lord." Another day, I said to him, "You know, David, you are a miracle." He quickly said back to me, "The Lord is the miracle, I am only a recipient."

What about Heather? I see her often because she is forever joined to our family by their child (my grandchild), Meghanne. Heather is inside of me; I love her like a daughter. I am seeing small breakthroughs, but nothing monumental yet. That is all right because I don't glory in appearances, I glory in the truth. God has promised her to me. As far as I am concerned, she is already saved because it is sealed by His promise in me. The reality will come in her, but I don't need to see it. For me, it is already there.

Life is pregnant with infinite possibilities desiring to be filled with Christ. We call these golden opportunities "problems." Let us now see that all our problems are really God's marvelous opportunities seeking fulfillment. Mark 11:23 says that whatsoever you desire, believe and you shall receive it. This is a tremendous promise and it is able to meet any problem. Nothing is impossible, so begin believing the ridiculous and laughing at the impossible.

26.

"Precious Seeds"

"He that goeth forth and weepeth, bearing precious seed, shall doubtless come again with rejoicing, bringing his sheaves with him. Except the Lord build the house, they labour in vain that build it"
(Psalms 126:6, 127:1)

Our son Danny has gone through hell with his wife. After five years of marriage, she walked out on him claiming she needed freedom to find herself. She was the love of his life so it has totally devastated him. Yet because of his pain, he is discovering who he is as Christ and becoming a giant of faith. When Cheri first left him, he asked the Lord to bring her home to him. Then the Lord showed him what he really wanted.

Now he says that by faith she will come home on the inside and discover who she is as a Christ person. If she comes back into their physical home, that will only be secondary and not the real point. Danny said to me the other day that in a sense, she had to do this, because how could she discover who she is until she first discovers who she is not. We are praising God for what he is making of Danny and Cheri by this suffering.

Cheri didn't come home to Danny's house, and it broke his heart. The only way to survive that kind of pain is to take it from the hand of God. It was a Cross for him, but he is totally resolved about it now. I have seen plenty of people in his same position living in blame, bitterness, unforgiveness, and resentment   I see none of that in Danny. Seeing **God only** in every situation will **always** heal us, and that it did.

That is why Jesus was so emphatic when he said, "If any man come after me let him take up his Cross." This simply means that we, like Danny, embrace our negative circumstances as from God. If we are holding on to (**my** life, **my** rights) or blaming the other person for hurting us, then we don't want to lay down our lives. It wasn't easy, but Danny took all this as from his Father. "All things are delivered unto me of my Father" (Matt. 11:27). That means **all**--even difficult spouses and impossible marriages.

Marriages are perfectly designed to bring out any form of self-centeredness. God does that by giving us our opposite. Opposite ways (I want my way, he wants his) opposite thoughts (I think this is right, he thinks that is right) and opposite desires (I want this, and he wants that). What a trick! Then to top it all off God traps us with the covenant promise of the marriage vows. What a perfect plan!

How can two opposite personalities with their own self interest in mind, live and love each other? Impossible! It is designed **not** to work. We all love the beautiful picture of marriage in Ephs.5:21-33.   We read it often at wedding ceremonies and rightly so. It is God's highest for us. "Wives be subject to your husbands, and husbands love your wives so much that you are willing to lay down your life for them." Perfect interchange of love, isn't it?

But how can this perfect pattern manifest itself in our lives when they are filled with so many warring opposites? And why doesn't it work?   I think the answer begins to manifest itself in another group of scriptures, spoken by Jesus in Luke 12:51: "Suppose ye that I am come to give **peace** on earth? I tell you, Nay; but rather **division**: For from henceforth there shall be five in one house divided, three against two, and two against three. The Father shall be divided against the son, and the son against the father; the mother against the daughter, and the daughter against the mother; the mother-in-law against her daughter-in-law, and the daughter-in-law against her mother-in-law." Now wait a minute Jesus, you tell us to love one another in one breath and then turn right around and promise us nothing but war and division?

Puzzling isn't it? Yet, if we know God's ways, we can begin to understand. The Ephesians 5:21 passage is the perfect picture of marriage, yet nothing is safe unless it goes to the **Cross**. That means a real death to a false self which thinks it wants its own way, and that death takes place in both partners. But at the start it only takes one person to die and rise in Christ, then that person can call the same into being for the other.

Harmony cannot be manifest in a marriage where self centeredness reigns in people. That has to be exposed. People have to be wounded to get to the root of self-centeredness, which has been carefully covered up by false righteousness. God wounds us, then He binds us up, but first the wounding must be severe and very radical or it won't have its lasting effect, for we will soon cover ourselves back up again in self-righteousness. Our identity has to be transformed. We must find ourselves as forms of God, and God has to find himself as us. That takes a heart transplant, which produces a total reversal in our consciousness. For only with the unconditional love expressed by Christ, through our emptiness and helplessness, can we ever hope to love our mates. Now the problem is that at this point too many people run from the pain (like Cheri did) instead of embracing it.

Our unyielding and obstinate mates are perfectly designed by God to expose any self-centered, independent self-life. Troubled marriages are meant to force us to trust in the power of the unseen Healer, who in Christ has already resolved all warring opposites and can fit them back together again in harmony.

It is only Christ dwelling and reigning within that can heal people, mend broken relationships, and reverse the destruction of ruined lives. For God has promised in Isaiah 53 that the chastisement of our peace was upon him; and with his stripes **we are healed**, because we are trusting **Him** to master us, as well as our mates. That is why we are comforted by Isaiah 9:6&7: "Unto us a son is given: and the government shall be upon **his shoulder**: and his name shall be called Wonderful, Counselor, The mighty God, The everlasting Father, The Prince of Peace. Of the increase of his government and peace there shall be no end."

  Danny lost his outer marriage, but gained his inner marriage with Christ for himself, and, by faith, for Cheri. The other day I went over to Danny's empty house only to find fullness in his heart. There is a picture with a verse on it hanging on the wall. Diane, his sister, lovingly crossed stitched it for him. It says, "They that sow in tears shall reap in joy. He that goeth forth and weepeth, **bearing precious seed,** shall doubtless come again with rejoicing, bringing his sheaves with him" (Psalms 126:5-6). The joy of the Lord has truly blessed my Danny with precious seeds for Cheri. Since he took the Cross and suffered loss, then she **will** experience spiritual advancement, that is a promise (John 12:24).

27.
Diane's "Joy" Bottle

"Count it all Joy my brethren, when you encounter various trials, knowing that the testing of your faith produces endurance. And let endurance have her perfect work, that you may be perfect, and complete lacking nothing."
(James 1:2-3)

Let me share a treasure from the life of my daughter, Diane. Diane was a naturally uninhibited child. At a very early age she found the Lord, and cut her spiritual teeth on the truths of who she was in Christ. She was a beautiful girl and married in her early twenties. Soon after her marriage she started to gain weight. Although it wasn't her main concern, she started a reducing program and trimmed down. Soon after that, she found out she was pregnant. Needless to say, her pregnancy didn't help her weight problem. So she tried again, this time with a different weight loss program.

This soon became a pattern in her life; she gained weight, and then she would lose weight. After many times of trying and failing, she gave up. It was clear to me that this was going to be her Romans Seven, "For that which I do I allow not; for what I would, that do I not; but what I hate, that do I." I was thankful and hurt at the same time. But I knew not to touch it.

After she gave up, self hatred began to overcome her. For the first time in her, life she hated herself. It would overcome her so much that she would eat and sleep as much as she could to drown out her depression. You can imagine what that did to her self image, as well as her body. She choose not to talk to me about it, and I respected her decision, because I knew that the Spirit would show her **His** word on the situation. We parents **cannot** be our children's Holy Spirit.

Even as a little child, she was taught by the Spirit in a pure way. She knew how to, as she would explain, "hold up a paper towel roll and just see God at the other end of it." She knew that keeping her eyes on Jesus would carry her through any problem she ever had. But what about this one? She kept holding her imaginary paper towel roll up and just focusing on Jesus, but as she said, "God poked holes in it." She didn't want to look to the left or to the right, because all she would see was her ugly fat, which led to more self-hatred.

Then one day the Lord asked her, "Diane, what do you see when you look through the holes in the paper towel roll?" She replied, "I see me, and I hate what I see." He said right back to her, "No, look again, it's **Me** you are seeing! What you hate is really an expression of **Me**! Hating yourself is really hating **Me**!" That broke her, as tears filled her eyes. Suddenly she remembered a story a strange boy had given her in High School. She had never fully understood it, but it rang true to her heart, so she kept it tucked away in her Bible.

The story went like this: "The other day, as my six-year-old daughter was watching me shave, she suddenly asked, 'Daddy, where does God live?' '**In a well,**' I answered absentmindedly. 'Oh Daddy!' Debbie voiced her disgust at such a silly answer. At breakfast my wife asked, 'What's this you've been telling Debbie about God living in a well?' 'In a well?' I frowned. Now why had I said that?

Then, all at once, a scene came to mind that had been hidden in my memory for over thirty years. It had taken place in the small town of Kielce, in southeastern Poland, where I had grown up. A band of passing gypsies had stopped at the well in our courtyard. I must have been about five at the time. One gypsy in particular, a giant of a man, fascinated me. He had pulled a bucketful of water from the well and was standing there, feet apart, drinking. Some of the water was running down his short-cropped, fiery beard, and his muscular hands held the large wooden pail to his lips as if it weighed no more than a teacup. When he had finished, he took off his multicolored silk scarf and mopped his face with it.

Then he leaned over and looked into the well. Curious, I tried to pull myself up the well's stone rim to see what he was peering at. The giant noticed me. He smiled and scooped me up in his arms. 'Do you know who lives down there?' he asked. I shook my head. 'God lives there,' he said. 'Look!' And he held me over the edge of the well. There, in the still, mirror-like water, I saw my own reflection. **'But that's me**!' 'Ah,' said the gypsy, gently setting me down, **'Now you know where God lives'.**" (Author unknown.)

Tears poured down her face as she read it. Could it really be true? The fat body that she hated was really a form of **God**. The Glory filled her heart that day. This was the beginning of the miracle of self-acceptance for her. The biggest miracle in the universe is for people to really love themselves as forms of Christ and experience the release of self-acceptance. The whole world walks in self-hatred, but my precious daughter caught the glory of Christ in her that day.

I heard a song by Evie Turnquist some time ago and this line grabbed me; "You can search for God in the Bible, or in Church, but until you find God in the mirror, you haven't found Him at all."

During her depression the Spirit comforted her with these verses: "My brethren, count it all **joy** when you fall into various temptations; knowing this, that the trying of your faith works patience. But let patience have her perfect work, that you may be perfect and complete, lacking nothing" (James 1:2-3).

She keeps a bottle of **"Joy"** dishwashing soap by her kitchen sink. It reminds her to "count it all joy" when she starts to feel pulled about herself. She, as it were, squirts a little "Joy" in her mess and it cleans it right up. So simple, but so true. Her faith counts her temptation "**all joy**," because it reminds her of the opposite, which she says about herself by faith.

She went through her time of faith training just as we practice something until it becomes our consciousness. So it is with faith's training ground. But like our earthly school days, graduation finally comes. Today, self-acceptance has manifested itself in her. Finally the day came when she put her Joy bottle back under the sink. She didn't need it anymore. The temptation to hate herself had been swallowed up and replaced with satisfying self-love.

Whether she loses weight or remains heavy isn't the point! The point is that she will forever know that her body is precious in the sight of the Lord, for it is an expression of **Him**. He is pleased to express himself through fat bodies, skinny bodies, and all in-between. Colossians 1:22 says, "In the body of His flesh through death, to present **you** holy, and unblameable, and unreproveable in his sight." Self-acceptance is the real miracle and far more important to discover than losing pounds. Weight loss is always temporary and secondary to the real point.

I asked her a question the other day, "Is it better for you to lose weight, or for you to love yourself just like you are and be able to help others find the miracle of self-acceptance?" Without hesitation she said, "It's better to help others."

28.

Susan, My Chariot of Fire

"While we look not at the things which are seen, but at the things which are not seen; for the things which are seen are temporal; but the things which are not seen are eternal. For we walk by faith, not by sight."
(2 Corinthians 4:18 & 5:7)

I guess my Susan is most like me, of all my children. She is fiery, independent, and unteachable. I am glad that I had my own life as my frame of reference for raising her, because it at least gave me understanding. Even so, the Lord has taught me a new thing about faith through her.

At birth Susan had numerous grand-mall seizures. Her doctor told me that she would probably be retarded. That was quite a blow, but I remember well my response, "I will **not** ask for outer deliverance Lord, Your will be done for only You know what glory you are going to get from her life." My mother came to visit me at the hospital soon after that, and her response was quite different. She said, "You can't ask? Well, O.K., but **I** can." And she did. Susan ended up with only a small amount of nerve damage and has never had a seizure since. Even her Jewish doctor was amazed.

One day, when Susan was only six years old, Pat Boone came on the television talking about Jesus. Susan stuck her finger in her mouth and said, "Gag, I hate that!"

Scott and I were devastated. Scott said to me, "No wonder she hates Jesus, that is **all you talk about!**" My soul went to hell. The very thing that I wanted her to have was repulsive to her and I was probably the cause. For about a week, I went crazy on the inside.

Then the Lord said to me, "If you believe that you are a stumbling block to her, then that is what you will produce, because what you believe is what you get. If I dare to believe that I am witnessing Jesus to her in my silence, then that is what I will bring into being." I grabbed at that word and kept my mouth shut about Jesus as much as I could. I believed she would learn to love Jesus in her own time and her own way, and I couldn't touch her Christian education. That was certainly different from the way I raised my other children. But it sure stretched my faith, which was the point.

By the time she approached her teens, she was very radical, outspoken, boy-crazy, cute (but insecure) and dyslexic. What a combination! If I would come down on her too much, she would threaten to run away. She was very active, so she didn't want to miss anything (other than school). I would take her to parties that I knew weren't what I would approve of, but if I didn't take her, I knew she would go anyway. So I decided it was safer to take her. I would drop her off and pray, "Lord your keeping power is far greater than what I can see, and I am praising you for it." I would say it over and over again. It gave me a measure of peace. Enough, anyway, to get me to the next stage of her life.

Then the Lord gave me a way to deal with her that seemed ridiculous, but I did it. He told me to tell her that **I trusted her.** I knew that was absurd, but I saw the wisdom behind it. She was going to rebel against me regardless of what I would tell her. Trusting her would put the responsibility on her and take the attention **away** from me telling her what to do. Then the Lord showed me that I was really calling her trustworthiness into being.

On Mount Carmel Elijah called rain into being when there was not a cloud in the sky. He sent a runner down to the seaside seven times to look for the rain cloud. It looked crazy, but he kept saying, "**it is there,** go down to the seaside and look for it." After the seventh time there was a small cloud way off in the distance. Elijah said, "**There it is**, get off the mountain immediately, for there is a great rain coming." It came so hard that it almost washed them off the mountain.

The Lord showed me to do that same thing with Susan. I insisted that trustworthiness was really inside of her, and I was going to believe it into being. I said to her, "I am going to **trust you.** That means that I am **not** going to police you on everything you do. If the Lord wants me to know what you are doing then He will tell me." It worked. I knew she was lying to me lots of times, but I always said that I trusted her. She started maturing and lying less and less. A year or so later, she told me that she would have been in "Maryhurst"(a home for troubled girls) if she hadn't had me for a mother. I take no credit. The Lord raised her, not me.

Then a precious thing happened. At her senior retreat share time, her dad and I were sitting on the first row wondering what in the world she would say. She got up before two hundred people with tears in her eyes. The retreat had really touched her. At the retreat, her best friend, who was depressed, told her that she sounded just like **"me."**

She stood up at the retreat and told two hundred people, and me especially, that for her whole life she **never** wanted to be like her mother, but she knew now that she really is like me. So now she wanted everyone to know that she was choosing the same path that I had chosen for my life. I'm not sure if anyone else knew what that meant, but I did. I was totally surprised, but I thought to myself, "She cannot make that word come into being, only the Lord can do that, so I will wait until he does it and not expect her be any different for now."

Susan is nineteen now. She still has some maturing to do, but she is learning how to believe God in every situation. I am proud of her. I love her fire, I wouldn't want that part of her to change for anything. God made her that way. The only change will be a redirection of her fire **His** way, instead of **her** way.

Oneness
by: Jacob Boehme

When the Spirit of Divine Love passed through my spirit, then my humanity and the divinity form but one single being, one single conception, and one single light. A thing that is "one" has neither commandment or law. Therefore, all that is to subsist in God must be freed from its own will. It must have no individual fire burning in it; but God's fire must be its fire. Its will must be united to God, that God and the will and spirit of man may be but one. For that which is one is not at enmity with itself, for it has only one will. wherever it goes, or whatever it does, all is one with it.

God dwells in all things; and nothing comprehends Him, unless it be one with Him. But if it go out from the one, it goes out of God into itself, and is other than God, and separates itself. And here it is that law arises, that it should proceed again out of itself into the One, or else remain separate from the One. And thus it may be known what is sin, or how it is sin. Namely, when the human will separates itself from God into an existence of its own, and awakens its own self, and burns in its own fire, which is not capable of the divine Fire.

Postscript

I will end this book the same way that I began it: "In this world, two prevailing unresolved problems confront mankind: man hates himself and man hates suffering." These two problems plague mankind and seem unanswerable. Hopefully, the Spirit has begun to give you His answers to these age-old problems. In this last chapter I will simply reiterate in capsulated form what I believe the answers to these questions are.

Christians all over the world are really hungry to know the mystery of "Christ in you." It is a wonderful blessing to know that we have a marvelous Savior living in us. However, it is a far deeper truth to know that we have an equally total and complete **self,** containing and expressing our wonderful Savior. Yet it is here that most Christians get snagged and even stopped. Most of us love and worship the Savior that saved us, but we hate the human self that He saved. There is something definitely very wrong with such a contradiction. Paul clears it up in Colossians 1:27-28. It says that we have a total Christ living His life in us. Verse 28 goes on to say that he (Paul) teaches and warns every man in all wisdom; that he might present every **man** perfect in Christ Jesus. A perfect Christ in a perfect man! What a revelation!

Now, how can we make such a statement about ourselves, when most of the time we feel there is a total Christ in us, yet there seems to be a condemned and failing **me**? Here lies the hidden root of our problem: the condemned and failing **me** is the false independent-self mentality we all inherited at the fall. This lying mentality (working in us as if it were the truth), is the source of our failure. We are blood-bought Christians, saved by grace, with Christ living in us. Yet we still have the delusions of Satan, our former owner. Our delusions are in the identity level of our consciousness, "who am I." We mistakenly think we have a strong and alive self, able to perform by our own resources. Therefore, when the Bible says, "Be ye holy as I am holy," we try our best to be so. If we are honest, we have to admit we are failing most of the time and this failure floods our consciousness with a false condemned image of a failing me. Paul had the same dilemma we do when he cried out in Romans 7:24, "O wretched **man that I am**, who can deliver me from this body of death."

The light came to Paul when he saw that the human being cannot produce good or evil of itself. The human is not a producer, but simply a receiver. The human is also a neutral being and not self-producing. This self-sufficient energy was indwelling sin in Paul's flesh members. The good news is that it was not the human Paul, it was Satan disguised as him.

By faith Paul could finally leap into the truth of who he really was. He could see himself at the cross, that is; "dead to sin/Satan, and alive to righteousness/Christ." He claimed his deliverance in the "bodily death and resurrection of Christ", which is the second work of the cross. He was crucified with Christ, and he, Paul, no longer lived, but Christ lived in him. Then the life of Christ could be expressed through him, as the human form of Paul.

What most Christians don't know is that there is a second operation of the cross that totally delivers us from this insidious lie that falsely holds us in captivity. Colossians 1:20 declares that the blood of Christ reconciles us back to God, and cleanses us from all our sins and gives us peace with God. However, in verse 22, Paul brings out the second operation of the Cross... "in the body of his flesh, he might present **you** holy, unblameable and unreproveable in his sight." It is one thing to know we are forgiven by faith in His precious blood, but it is a far deeper level of knowing to know that **we** are holy, total, and complete.

The cross of Christ has already set us free from self-condemnation (Romans 8:1), and made us partakers of the "divine nature" (II Peter 1:3-4). And by a simple work of faith, embracing these promises, we can enter into this promised oneness. There is nothing left for us to do, just believe these promises by faith. I Thess. 5:24 says, "Faithful is He that calleth you. He also will do it."

Miraculously, we can begin to accept our negative reactions as right and not try to get out of them. We can begin to (go with) our negatives instead of trying to conquer them, knowing they are right and simply springboards to faith. All the things we have hated about ourselves and considered liabilities now become our greatest assets. The cross transmutes our flesh into right spirit-use. The perfect Oneness that Jesus prophetically declared in John 17:21-23, "I in them, and thou in me, that they may be made perfected in oneness," bursts into being as a living reality in us today.

We now understand that it is through suffering that we inherit these promises. II Timothy 2:12 says, "If we **suffer**, we shall also **reign with him.**" Hebrews 6:12 says, "through faith and patience, we inherit the promises." And, I Peter 5:10 says, "After you have suffered a while, make you **perfect** establish, strengthen, settle you." The greatest victory chapter in the bible is Romans 8. Yet, it is filled with suffering. Victory and suffering are the opposite ends of the same thing...just like light and darkness, life and death, chaos and calm. All reality is two-fold in nature, manifesting itself by its hidden opposite. It is impossible for the "no condemnation" victory of Romans 8 to come as a living reality in us, except by the painful suffering of Romans 7. Both are necessary opposite ends of the same reality.

If we can dare accept the fact that God means evil, and purposes it for our good, we will begin to see that there is only one Person in the universe, and that one Person is the God of infinite unconditional love. Then all the negatives in our lives are experienced as acts of love and redemptive in nature. The unresolved opposites are resolved into the single eye of seeing God Only. I Cor. 13:10 says that when the perfect is come the partial is done away with. When we see in part, we are just that, partial. But when all is seen as a loving whole, then the perfect is come and we come home inside of ourselves.

Let me end by saying that I am praying that God will reveal these liberating secrets to you, for He promises, "You **shall** know the truth, and the truth **shall** set you **free**." May God bless you, and my love is with you all.

If anyone has any questions or comments concerning this book, please write me:

**Sylvia Pearce
P.O. Box 43268
Louisville, Kentucky 40253
USA
502-245-4581
sylviap@theliberatingsecret.org**

There are two places that you can find these union truths on the Internet: http://www.theliberatingsecret.org, and http://www.spiritradio.net. The Liberating Secret.org is our primary literary web-site, while Spirit Radio.net, or currently named, Spirit Broadcasting Network is our internet TV and radio station on the air 24 hours a day broadcasting these liberating truths.

Also, if you might want more copies of this book, please write me at the above address. Or visit our book store on the web-site where you will find many other books, CD's, DVD's, and audio tapes.